BEHIND BARS

True Crime Stories of
WHISKEY HEISTS, BEER BANDITS, and FAKE MILLION-DOLLAR WINES

MIKE GERRARD

Prometheus Books
Essex, Connecticut

Prometheus Books

An imprint of The Globe Pequot Publishing Group, Inc.
64 South Main Street
Essex, Connecticut 06426
www.globepequot.com

Distributed by NATIONAL BOOK NETWORK

British Library Cataloguing in Publication Information Available

Library of Congress Cataloging-in-Publication Data

Names: Gerrard, Mike, 1949– author.
Title: Behind bars : true crime stories of whiskey heists, beer bandits, and fake million-dollar wines / Mike Gerrard.
Description: Lanham, MD : Prometheus, [2024] | Includes bibliographical references. | Summary: "Award-winning travel and drinks writer Mike Gerrard takes readers on a centuries-long journey highlighting the most bizarre—and expensive—alcohol-related crimes all while revealing the inside world of booze: how it has been distilled, legislated, imbibed, and infused into culture and society for hundreds of years"—Provided by publisher.
Identifiers: LCCN 2024009671 (print) | LCCN 2024009672 (ebook) | ISBN 9781493084418 (paperback) | ISBN 9781493084425 (epub) Subjects: LCSH: Drinking of alcoholic beverages—United States. | Alcoholism and crime—United States. | Alcoholic beverage law violations—United States.
Classification: LCC HV5292 .G47 2024 (print) | LCC HV5292 (ebook) | DDC 362.2920973—dc23/eng/20240412
LC record available at https://lccn.loc.gov/2024009671
LC ebook record available at https://lccn.loc.gov/2024009672

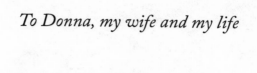

To Donna, my wife and my life

Contents

INTRODUCTION

It's thought that alcohol was first made in China in about 7000 BCE, and it's highly likely that alcohol was first stolen in China a few days later. Alcohol attracts thieves, fakers, and scammers, though, surprisingly, the most popular item stolen from grocery stores is cheese. Slipping a package of parmesan into your pocket, though, is somehow not as audacious as walking into a liquor store empty-handed and walking out with a $26,000 bottle of fifty-year-old Glenfiddich single malt, as one guy did in Toronto in 2013. No wonder he smirked at the security camera as he strolled through the door.

A connection has always existed between booze and crime. The earliest example in *Behind Bars* dates to 79 CE in Pompeii, Italy, where the ash from the erupting Mount Vesuvius preserved the sleight of hand of the local wine merchants for all eternity. More recent cases are up-to-date and ongoing, with criminals awaiting sentencing or in some cases still at large.

In chapter 1, we start by examining the origins of today's immense Scottish whiskey industry, which in 2022 was worth £7.1 billion ($8.95 billion) to the UK economy. Its building blocks were the illicit stills, hidden in glens and in basements, buried underground, and concealed behind waterfalls. Some of those illegal distillers eventually became legal, leading to the founding of brands we still know today, like the Glenlivet. The ongoing battles between distillers and excisemen are often hilarious and occasionally tragic, like the story of the exciseman who was hanged for forgery because his wages couldn't feed his family.

Chapter 2 begins in Scotland and travels with a whiskey smuggler and rum-runner to the Caribbean and then to the shores of the United States, where ships dropped anchor just outside US territorial waters.

From there, under the frustrated gaze of the US Coast Guard, they sold wine and spirits to thirsty US citizens during Prohibition. We also learn how rum shipped from Cuba to Honduras ended up in Louisiana and along the US southern and eastern coasts.

Chapter 3 explores the murky world of moonshine from Alaska to Alabama but most notably in Kentucky, Virginia, and the Carolinas. We meet larger-than-life moonshiners like Popcorn Sutton, Alvin Sawyer (the teetotal moonshine king of the Great Dismal Swamp), and Percy Flowers, who made $1 million a year, tax free, producing moonshine. We also learn how some of the best early NASCAR drivers, like Junior Johnson, honed their skills driving souped-up cars transporting moonshine on back roads in the dead of night.

Chapter 4 explains why Percy Flowers earned $1 million a year and why liquor from Scotland and Cuba was in demand off the coast of the United States: Prohibition. We meet Al Capone, his Canadian counterpart Rocco Perri, and Perri's partner in crime, Bessie Starkman, the most notorious female gangster in Canadian history, and uncover the White House's supplier of wine and spirits during Prohibition and presidential attitudes toward Prohibition.

In chapter 5, we learn about some of the most audacious liquor heists in history: from the lone individual who walked into a liquor store and walked out with whiskey worth tens of thousands of dollars to the organized gangs who broke into wine cellars—through front doors, the buildings next door, or even the catacombs of Paris—and made off with millions in fine wines. We also meet the audacious young couple who infiltrated one of the best wine cellars in Spain simply by borrowing the key while ordering dessert in the middle of the night. It's amazing how many bottles of rare wine you can fit into a backpack.

Chapter 6 tells the short but shameful story of the Whiskey Ring scandal. In the span of five years, a conspiracy of government agents, politicians, whiskey distillers, and distributors managed to defraud the government of today's equivalent of $83 million in liquor taxes. The ringleader? A revenue collector who decided to collect revenue for himself.

In chapter 7, we investigate the shadowy world of wine and whiskey investment schemes, particularly the ones that aren't what they seem.

Get advice about scam investments in wines and whiskeys that don't exist, and read about the scammers who spend their millions on flashy sports cars, international travel, and, in one guy's case, women on dating websites.

Finally, we look at the fake stuff—not the nonexistent bottles sold by scammers, but the bottles of wine and whiskey whose contents don't reflect what's on the label. Labels that indicate $50 champagne but contain $2 Italian prosecco; Johnnie Walker bottles filled with rubbing alcohol or even dirty water; the finest French Bordeaux that's actually Spanish plonk.

We end with the greatest wine fraudster of them all, the Indonesian immigrant to the United States who became one of the world's leading experts in the most expensive burgundy wines on earth. He lived the high life, bought Lamborghinis, and made millions buying and selling bottles of some of the most expensive wines on the planet. The problem was that many of the wines he sold contained not nineteenth-century French burgundy but twenty-first-century wine from Napa Valley.

At the end of this book, an appendix includes the legal definitions of various wines and spirits to help you read labels more accurately—assuming the label accurately reflects what's inside the bottle. What's the difference between bourbon and straight bourbon? How long is Scottish whiskey required to age compared to Canadian whiskey or American bourbon? What does a tequila label tell you, and what constitutes real champagne? Hopefully by the end of this book, you'll be educated as well as entertained. Hopefully, also, you won't be offended if you're from Scotland or Canada. For the sake of consistency, I've gone for the "whiskey" spelling rather than "whisky."

· 1 ·

SCOTLAND'S ILLICIT STILLS

The tax revenue due on whiskey sitting in bonded warehouses in Scotland—roughly twelve billion bottles—is worth more than the United Kingdom's entire gold reserves held at the Bank of England. It's hardly surprising, then, that illicit distilling is and always has been frowned upon by governments. Equally, the first attempts at taxing whiskey, which was seen by Scottish farmers as a legitimate and harmless way of using surplus grains, were more than frowned upon by the whiskey makers. Farmers regarded making whiskey from their own barley as just the same as making porridge from their own oats, so why should it be taxed? What next—pay tax on their breakfast porridge? Little wonder it resulted in mayhem and murder.

The oldest written reference about distilling in Scotland dates to 1494. That was the year that King James IV of Scotland commissioned John Cor, a monk at Lindores Abbey, to turn eight bolls of malt into aqua vitae, the water of life, the origins of whiskey. A boll was a Scottish unit for measuring capacity. Because two different bols were used depending on what was being measured and because different regions had different definitions of a bol, it's hard to determine just how much eight bols was. A good guess, though, would be about 1,700 liters, so a fair amount of whiskey.

This is the oldest written reference to distilling in Scotland, and it proves that the monks of Lindores Abbey were indeed distilling spirits way back then. So were many others, of course, and it probably had been occurring for a few centuries, but no one has written proof that they were doing so in Scotland before 1494. Contrary to popular belief,

HOW TO TURN BARLEY INTO WHISKEY

Making whiskey from barley involves several key steps, including malting, mashing, fermenting, distilling, and aging. Here's a basic outline of the process:

1. Malting: Barley grains are soaked in water to initiate germination. During germination, enzymes are activated, which convert starches in the barley into fermentable sugars. The germinated barley, known as malt, is then dried in a kiln to halt the germination process.

2. Mashing: The malted barley is ground into a coarse powder called grist. The grist is mixed with hot water in a large vessel called a mash tun. This process, known as mashing, allows the enzymes in the malt to further break down the starches into sugars, creating a sugary liquid called wort.

3. Fermentation: The wort is transferred to fermentation vessels, typically made of stainless steel or wood. Yeast is added to the wort, and fermentation begins. During fermentation, yeast converts the sugars in the wort into alcohol and carbon dioxide. This process usually takes several days to complete.

4. Distillation: Once fermentation is complete, the fermented liquid, known as "wash" or "beer," is distilled in a still. The wash is heated in the still, and the alcohol vaporizes at a lower temperature than water, allowing it to be separated and collected. This process is typically performed in two or more distillation runs to increase the alcohol content and remove impurities.

5. Aging: Finally, it's common for the spirit to be aged in a barrel to add flavor and color, but the rules governing this (if any) vary from country to country. See the appendix for more information.

the Scots did not invent whiskey (but don't say this in a Glasgow bar on a Saturday night). It was probably introduced to Scotland from Ireland by monks in the fifth century. Nor did the Scots invent the kilt or the bagpipes, but that's another story.

Soon after this, in the sixteenth century, the first known prosecution for illicit distilling took place. The guilty person was a woman, Bessie Campbell. This isn't so surprising; for a long time, distilling was seen as a domestic chore. As far back as in ancient Egypt, the work was divided so that men went out to labor and the women stayed home and produced the family's food and drink. Distilling was seen as the equivalent of cooking, traditionally a woman's role. In addition to wives, widows, single women, and female servants were included among Scotland's illicit distillers.

Women also proved to be adept at distracting the excisemen, or gaugers, as they were called, when they came to look for signs of illegal distilling. On seeing a gauger approach, one woman hastily wrapped a barrel of whiskey in blankets, put it in a cradle, and sang to it while the gauger searched the rest of the premises without success. Another woman leaped into bed and pretended to be in labor when the gaugers turned up. The husband said he would go in search of a midwife if the gaugers stayed with his wife, but the nervous gaugers preferred instead to go for the midwife themselves, leaving the couple to clear away all signs of their distilling activities. When the gaugers returned with the midwife, the woman declared it to be a false alarm, and the gaugers searched the house in vain.

On another occasion, on the island of Eigg, a distiller was warned that the gaugers had landed. He was in possession of an illegal cask of whiskey, so he hid it beneath the bed while his wife climbed under the blankets. When the gauger arrived, he was told that the wife had given birth two days previously. He apologized for disturbing her and left her alone, finding nothing in the rest of the house.

On the island of Jura, Islay's little neighbor, the story is told of two brothers who were illicit distillers. They had a cask of illegal whiskey in their house when they heard that the gaugers were in the neighborhood, having come from Islay on the ferry. There were no resident excisemen on Jura, and those who lived on Islay had trouble getting to

Jura undetected. The brothers put the cask close to the fire and got their mother to sit on it, concealing it with her voluminous skirts. Invited in all innocence to search the house, the gaugers found nothing and left.

Women were also involved in the smuggling as well as the making of spirits. They hid bottles and even small barrels under their skirts, knowing they wouldn't be searched by customs officers. Well, not usually, though it did happen. Groups of women would collect consignments of spirits wearing loose clothing, only to return with their dresses much tighter.

The story of illicit distilling, though, is as much about the gaugers as the distillers, and we can learn a lot about the gauger's life from the book *The Memorial and Case of Malcolm Gillespie* (1828). Gillespie's memoir was published posthumously; he was one of the few excisemen to die on the scaffold. Gillespie became an exciseman in 1799 and was first based in Prestonpans, about eight miles east of Edinburgh on the Firth of Forth. Here he distinguished himself by investigating the local salt trade and discovering evidence of fraud. Ironically, the crime for which Gillespie was ultimately hanged was forgery.

By 1812, he had been promoted and had encountered his first dealings with illicit whiskey making and smuggling while responsible for a large area on Deeside, with the River Don on one side and the River Dee on the other, inland from Aberdeen, the largest port in northeast Scotland. It was a place where distillers—or their smuggling agents—could discretely buy empty barrels without attracting attention and where full barrels could be shipped out.

To help in his battles with smugglers, he bought a ferocious bull terrier. He trained the dog to bite the smugglers' horses on the nose, causing them to lose their cargo of illicit whiskey. The dog met his end when he was shot and killed by a smuggler. Gillespie, who also had been shot on more than one occasion, was pretty ferocious himself. Once, he took on a gang of about thirty smugglers with the aid of just one assistant. He survived only because additional excise officers and a group of local militia arrived to save the day—and their boss.

Gaugers had a financial incentive to find smugglers and distillers, since they personally received a half share of whatever was confiscated, the other half going to the government. Although they also received a small salary, gaugers were responsible for paying all the expenses of their office and for paying their staff. They incurred other expenses, as Gillespie reveals in his autobiography:

> in a country where the inhabitants are almost wholly connected with the illicit trade, it is difficult to find a person among them who can be prevailed upon to give information against his neighbour and nothing short of the Officer's Share of the Seizure can induce the informant to divulge his secret. It has principally been in this way that I have involved myself in debt.

Gillespie explains that he often lost money in these endeavors, even when recovering large amounts of illicit whiskey. In addition, he had been wounded forty-two times, and, during his twenty-eight years with the excisemen, he had recovered more than 20,000 gallons (91,000 liters) of spirit and 60,000 gallons of wash (273,000 liters) while raiding 407 stills. One still he seized had a capacity to produce 50 gallons of whiskey at a time, and Gillespie found 300 gallons of wash there.

This still was in Skene, only eight miles west of Aberdeen, and Gillespie describes it as "so constructed that a person even of no ordinary penetration could scarcely be able to find it out, although within a few yards."

Despite his successes, Gillespie found himself in debt, which led to his downfall. He had a wife and children to support, and in 1827 he was arrested for forging treasury bills. This was a capital offense at that time, and Gillespie was hanged on November 15, 1827. A Parliamentary inquiry into smuggling in 1736 shows the violent nature of the gauger's job, which revealed that more than 250 officers had been beaten, abused, or wounded and 6 killed since Christmas 1723.

Three years before Gillespie became an exciseman, the most famous exciseman of all time passed away: the poet Robert Burns. Burns was born January 25, 1759, a date that is now celebrated worldwide as Burns Night, a celebration during which more whiskey is probably drunk than on any other night of the year. Burns was the eldest of seven children and worked alongside his brothers on the family farm in Ayrshire. Because of the family's poverty, Burns was primarily taught by his father, though he and a brother were fortunate enough to also have a tutor, who kindled Burns's interest in literature.

At the age of fifteen, Burns started writing poetry, but he was twenty-seven before his first collection was published. This was at a time when he was seeking to immigrate to Jamaica to take a job on a sugar plantation but lacked the funds to pay for his passage. The book was an immediate success, and Burns decided to stay in Scotland. Two years later, he married, moved to Dumfriesshire, and took a job as a trainee exciseman. Although his poems made him famous, they didn't make him rich.

Though much of Burns's work as an exciseman was office based and involved writing reports, he also undertook many long journeys on horseback in wet weather. His job, for which he was paid £50 a year (about £4,700/$6,000 today), required him to ride as much as forty miles a day, five days a week, in order to cover the area he was responsible

ROBERT BURNS

Robert Burns wrote a poem about Scotland's illicit whiskey makers titled "The Deil's Awa wi' the Exciseman" (The Devil's Away with the Exciseman). In it, Burns expresses his disdain for the excise officers like himself who were responsible for collecting taxes on goods such as alcohol, including those that were smuggled or produced illegally. Here are the first few lines of the poem:

The Deil cam fiddlin' thro' the town,
And danc'd awa wi' th' Exciseman,
And ilka wife cries, "Auld Mahoun
I wish you luck o' the prize, man."

The poem goes on to describe how the townsfolk celebrate the departure of the exciseman, suggesting their support for smuggling and opposition to the enforcement of excise laws.

for. This undoubtedly contributed to the ill health he already suffered, probably brought on by arduous farm labor from an early age. He also had a rheumatic heart condition.

He died on July 21, 1796, on the day his wife gave birth to their son Maxwell, who would die before his third birthday. A ladies' man, Burns fathered nine children with his wife, three by other women, and probably others not known. He didn't have any direct involvement in the discovery of illicit stills, although he was involved in a risky encounter with smugglers, as described in the next chapter.

As well as his fondness for the ladies, Burns also enjoyed a wee dram—or two. He opposed taxes on whiskey, as several of his poems make clear. It seems strange, then, that he should have worked as an excise officer. However, he was a man of contradictions, and he needed to earn a living somehow. When he applied for the job, the farm on which he was living was operating at a loss. From childhood onward, Burns feared financial insecurity, which deeply affected his life.

He wrote poems critical of excisemen, and his political activity certainly conflicted with his job. He once received a warning from his superiors about his political conduct, although they can't have been too annoyed with him, since he was promoted soon afterward. The conflict between his job and his beliefs continued to plague him and led to fits of depression, to which he had been prone all his life.

━━━◆━━━

The first attempts to restrict distilling in Scotland were made with good intentions. In 1579, when it looked like there would be a poor harvest, the Scottish government banned the making and selling of spirits from December 1579 until October 1580 to help with the food supply, though ten months was obviously a long time for a Scotsman to go without his wee dram. Periodically, the ban was reimposed whenever there was the prospect of a poor harvest and not enough food to go around.

It was in 1643, though, when the trouble really began. That was the year that the English government imposed the first tax on the making of spirits, as well as on tobacco and some other goods. The tax was to raise money to fund the parliamentary armies during the English Civil War, and it was the start of the excise system. The Scottish government followed suit the following year, because it also had armies to pay for in support of the English parliamentary forces. Taxing whiskey—or aqua vitae as it was called—and other strong liquors was an excellent way of raising money.

The Scottish government taxed every pint of spirit at 2 shillings and 8 pence (13 pence/16 cents in today's currency), a considerable amount almost four hundred years ago, even though a Scottish pint then was equivalent to almost a half gallon today. For farmers who were not wealthy and mostly making spirits for family and friends, this was not popular. In addition to the whiskey produced, a byproduct of the process was winter feed for their cattle. The result, not surprisingly, was an upsurge in both smuggling and illicit stills.

Strangely enough, when the Civil War ended in 1651, the taxes didn't end with it. In fact, they expanded, setting the precedent for all governments everywhere. In 1688 a new act was passed that taxed imported liquor according to its strength. *Hooray*, said both patriots and smugglers alike. Then in 1699 the law was extended to homemade liquor too. *Boo*, said everyone except the smugglers and the illicit distillers, who by now were doing a roaring trade. Raise the price of legal liquor? Bring it on!

On top of all this, in 1697 England introduced a malt tax, which affected both brewers and distillers. This was seen as unfair, as it taxed one of the prime ingredients of both beer and whiskey and then the beer and whiskey made from the malt. How long before they started taxing the water used in the drinks?

In 1707 the stakes—and taxes—were raised even more when, first, the Act of Union was passed, bringing England and Scotland together to create the united kingdom known as Great Britain. This meant that English customs officers could work in Scotland to help combat both the smuggling and the illegal distilling. In fact, the Scottish Excise Board, which was established in Edinburgh in the wake of the act, was manned exclusively by Englishmen.

The second significant factor that occurred in 1707 was a considerable increase in the tax on alcohol. The governments clearly had no sense of irony (or shame): during a period of welcome peace, they increased a tax that had been levied to pay for a war. You can't really blame people for defying it. And defy it they did.

In 1713 the English Malt Tax was extended to Scotland, and even though it was half the rate the English paid, it caused major consequences north of the border. Till this point, the most popular drink in Scotland had not been whiskey but ale. In fact, it had been rather too popular, in the government's opinion, as one of the reasons for extending the tax to Scotland was to try to control the excessive drinking of ale. It worked—sort of. When it shot up in price or the quality dropped, people stopped drinking ale and started drinking illicit whiskey instead.

WHAT'S THE DIFFERENCE BETWEEN BEER AND ALE?

The terms "beer" and "ale" are often used interchangeably, but historically, there has been a distinction between the two. Nowadays, the difference between beer and ale is mainly based on their brewing methods, ingredients, and fermentation characteristics.

Ingredients: Both beer and ale are brewed using similar ingredients, including water, malted barley (or other grains), hops, and yeast. However, the types of malt and hops used can vary depending on the specific style being brewed.

Fermentation: The primary difference between beer and ale lies in the type of yeast used and the fermentation process. Ales are brewed using top-fermenting yeast strains, which ferment at warmer temperatures (typically between 60°–75°F or 15°–24°C). This results in a faster fermentation process and produces fruity and complex flavors. Beers, on the other hand, can be brewed using either top-fermenting or bottom-fermenting yeast strains. Bottom-fermenting yeast strains ferment at cooler temperatures (around

45°–55°F or 7°–13°C) and settle at the bottom of the fermentation vessel. This slower fermentation process typically results in cleaner and crisper flavors associated with lagers.

Styles: Ales encompass a wide range of beer styles, including pale ales, India pale ales (IPAs), stouts, porters, wheat beers, and Belgian ales, among others. Beers include lagers, pilsners, bocks, Märzens, and other styles that are fermented with bottom-fermenting yeast.

Characteristics: Ales generally have a more pronounced malt character, with fruity esters and sometimes a higher alcohol content. Beers tend to be lighter and crisper, with a cleaner fermentation profile and lower alcohol content compared to ales.

Although the terms "beer" and "ale" have historically referred to different types of fermented beverages, the distinction has become less significant in modern brewing terminology. Both terms are often used interchangeably to refer to a wide variety of fermented grain-based beverages, and the distinction between them is primarily based on the specific brewing process and yeast used.

The situation grew worse in 1725, when the Scottish malt tax was doubled to bring it in line with the rate paid in England. Brewers in Edinburgh stopped brewing as a protest measure. Rioting began in Hamilton, fifteen miles southeast of Glasgow, and spread throughout the country, including in Edinburgh, Ayr, Dundee, and Stirling. It was at its worst in Glasgow, though, where eleven people were killed in what became known as the Shawfield riots, or the malt tax riots.

By the 1760s, illicit stills were responsible for producing an estimated 500,000 gallons of whiskey each year, ten times the amount of legal whiskey. In 1777, there were said to be four hundred unlicensed stills in Edinburgh, compared to only eight legal ones. The city's population at the time was around 70,000, so there was a still—legal or illegal—for every 172 people. The equivalent today would be more than three thousand stills. Coincidentally, the number of legal distilleries in Edinburgh today is about the same as it was in 1777.

Around the same time, there were thought to be anywhere from three hundred to five hundred illicit stills in Glasgow, many of them around Saltmarket Place. In January 1815, ten stills were raided and closed in the Saltmarket area alone. This number was matched by large numbers of illegal drinking dens, a kind of alcoholic equivalent of today's farm-to-table approach to dining.

Drinking dens like this were commonplace in Scottish cities right up until the 1970s, when changes in liquor laws and the boom in supermarkets providing cheap spirits led to their gradual disappearance. This is probably just as well. One investigation in the 1870s analyzed thirty examples of spirits from a range of Scottish drinking dens. Only two of the thirty samples proved to be straightforward, unadulterated whiskey. The others included methylated spirits, varnish, turpentine, and sulfuric acid. And some people think bottom-shelf spirits taste rough. In Glasgow in 1949, eight people died at a Hogmanay party after drinking illicit alcohol.

Meanwhile, back in 1781, private distilling was finally made illegal. Until that point, anyone could distill spirits for their own use, though it was illegal to sell them. Thus, distilling that had been done openly, for personal use, was driven underground. Literally so in many cases, since some people built underground bunkers in which to hide their stills.

The discovery of one such example was described by author Samuel Morewood in *An Essay on the Inventions and Customs in the Use of Inebriating Liquors* (1824):

> Perceiving, however, some brambles loosely scattered about the place, he proceeded, to examine more minutely, and on their removal, discovered some loose sods, under which was found a trap door leading to a small cavern, at the bottom of which was a complete distillery at full work, supplied by a subterranean stream, and the smoke conveyed from it through the windings of a tube that was made to communicate with the funnel of the chimney of the distillers' dwelling-house, situated at a considerable distance.

Housing your distillery underground is not without its hazards, as one distiller discovered when a cow fell in on him. A group of distillers operating near Kinnaird Castle in Angus found a different but ingenious hiding place for their equipment: a cave behind a waterfall. All went well until the waterfall swelled to twice its normal size after an unusually large winter thaw. The cave flooded, washing out the equipment, including filled barrels, which either smashed on the rocks below or bobbed downstream till some lucky individual found them.

To help with the clampdown on illegal distilling, the government offered a bounty of 1 shilling and 6 pence (10 cents) for information leading to the discovery of an illicit still. In the following year, a total of 1,940 stills were discovered. It sounds impressive; however, a number of distillers revealed the whereabouts of their own stills in order to acquire the reward money and buy better equipment.

In 1787, it's reckoned that 300,000 gallons of whiskey were smuggled across the border into England, demonstrating that the clampdown wasn't exactly effective. Moreover, more whiskey was being smuggled into continental Europe, and the majority was still being consumed within the borders of Scotland itself. Estimates of illegal production of 500,000 gallons a year might be conservative.

Then in 1795, Britain went to war with France—and excise duty on spirits immediately tripled. In 1799, the prime minister, William Pitt the Younger, introduced yet another new tax to help pay for the ongoing conflicts with France: income tax. This was in addition to a newly introduced inheritance tax. Little wonder that people felt taxed to the hilt. They paid tax if they bought barley; they paid tax if they made whiskey with it; now they also paid tax on the income made from selling the whiskey. Finally, when they died, their descendants paid tax on any money left over.

Then the Napoleonic Wars broke out in 1803, and Britain went into a recession. For many in the remote Highlands, where legitimate sources of income were negatively affected, illicit distilling became one of the few means that many families had of earning money. Their choice was to break the law or starve, and most people didn't agree with the law in the first place. Distilling spirits had always been seen as a pleasurable perk and a way of earning a little money on the side. Who were politicians to say that this centuries-old tradition was suddenly illegal? As the Scottish food historian F. Marian McNeill has written: "Once upon a time it was as natural for a Highlander to make whiskey as for a Frenchman to make wine."

In the late eighteenth and early nineteenth centuries, the whole situation was a mess. The continual increases in duty on legal spirits didn't help, serving only to make the illegal kind more attractive. So punitive were the duty increases that Ardbeg, which started distilling in 1798 and is now one of the most famous names in whiskey making on the island of Islay, went bankrupt in 1838. And in Campbeltown, today one of Scotland's five defined whiskey regions, there was virtually no legal distilling despite a thriving trade in illicit spirits. On the tiny island of Tiree in the Inner Hebrides, the two legal distilleries both went out of business during this period, yet somehow the island continued to produce as much whiskey as before.

This situation was summed up by Dr. John Leyden in his 1800 book *Journal of a Tour in the Highlands and Islands of Western Scotland* as quoted in Gavin D. Smith's excellent book, *The Secret Still*:

The distillation of whiskey presents an irresistible temptation to the poorer classes, as the boll of barley, which costs thirty shillings, produces by this process, between five and six guineas. This distillation had a most ruinous effect in increasing the scarcity of grain last year, particularly in Isla [*sic*] and Tiree, where the people subsisted chiefly on fish and potatoes.

An example from Tiree shows how adept the distillers were at dealing with the excisemen. One distiller, whose pot still leaked, saw the exciseman approaching, so he engaged him in conversation. The exciseman offered a reward if the distiller pointed him toward any illicit stills. The distiller said he didn't want to get anyone into trouble, and the exciseman explained that he would smash the still and ask no questions about its owner. The leaky still was smashed, the reward given, and the distiller immediately purchased a brand-new still.

The story of Campbeltown is worth a special diversion, just as the beautiful Kintyre peninsula, where it's located, is well worth a physical diversion if you're anywhere nearby. The first printed record of distilling in Campbeltown from 1636 served as confirmation that the rent for a farm was payable by supplying six quarts of aqua vitae. By 1792, twenty-two licensed distilleries were recorded in Campbeltown, an impressive number given that the population at that time was less than nine thousand.

That was soon to come to an end just five years later in 1797, when excise duties were vastly increased. Legal distilleries began to close, and for the next twenty years, there was no legal distilling in Campbeltown. There was still plenty of whiskey available, of course. In this respect, Campbeltown was a microcosm of what was happening across Scotland. Legal distillers, having paid huge amounts of money to obtain their licenses, were forced out of business by the punitive excise duties, only to continue to use their skills—and their stills—illegally.

We know a lot about what happened in Campbeltown thanks to the survival of the accounts of Robert Armour. Armour was a Campbeltown plumber and still maker who kept records from 1811 to 1817 of whom he supplied stills to and whether they were legal distilleries. One such legal distillery was John Beath and Company, which opened in 1817, becoming the town's first legal distillery in twenty years. However, Armour's records show that he was supplying Beath with stills long before that; presumably, the distiller had been making whiskey illicitly before going legal.

Armour's records also show that he made stills not just in Campbeltown, but for distillers as far afield as the islands of Gigha and Arran (one writer described Arran whiskies as "the burgundy of the vintages"). According to his books, members of Armour's family were involved in distilling, both legally and illegally, and among his customers were reputable locals including butchers, farmers, and innkeepers. Distillers could kit themselves out with a still for a relatively modest £5 (about £500/$630 today). The cost of the still could be recouped after the sale of about 10 gallons of whiskey.

Despite this craziness, the government continued with its relentless, short-sighted policy of simply increasing duties. In 1819, for example, it doubled the duty on the purchase of barley, which sent some of the barley trade underground as well as further increasing the number of illicit stills.

The government undermined its own efforts over and over again, losing revenue from sales of new distillery licenses, from existing distilleries going out of business, from lower legal barley purchases, and of course from lower legal whiskey sales. For example, in 1819 there were fifty-seven legal distilleries in the Scottish Highlands. Four years later there were forty-two, a decrease of 26 percent. In Scotland in 1820, there were almost five thousand prosecutions for illegal distilling, and by 1822 that figure had increased by around 25 percent. The number of prosecutions was only the tip of the illicit distilling iceberg: if five thousand distillers had been caught and the number of illegal stills continued to grow, imagine the overall scale of the operation. During the 1820s, the seizure of illicit stills increased to around fourteen thousand a year, according to estimates.

By 1823, the government finally recognized the problems it created by continually increasing excise duties and introduced what whiskey expert Gavin D. Smith describes as "the most far-reaching piece of excise legislation in British history." This was the Excise Act, which was a complete about-face on what, till then, had been government policy. Yes, even back then, governments made U-turns.

The 1823 Excise Act set the cost of a distilling license at £10, which is close to £1,500 ($1,900) levied today. The act also reduced duty on spirits by more than 50 percent, the government finally realizing that with every increase in the cost of legal whiskey, the illegal kind became that much more attractive. Because legal whiskey distillers had also been improving their techniques in order to make their spirit more appealing than the whiskey equivalent of bathtub gin, the 1823 act saw an increase in legal whiskey sales and of new legal distilleries. Many licensed distilleries grew from formerly illicit operations.

In fact, the first license for a new distillery issued after the act was to George Smith in 1824. An illicit distiller, he decided to take the legal route and founded the distillery that eventually became the Glenlivet. This was the first step in transforming Glenlivet (the glen, that is) from a hotbed of illicit activity to one of the most famous glens on Speyside and a name known around the world.

Other names followed, including Lochnagar, Aberlour, and Macallan. In Campbeltown from 1823 till 1837, at least twenty-seven new legal distilleries opened, while Islay was well on its way to becoming Scotland's whiskey island with six distilleries opening in the six years from 1824 to 1830.

Estimates from the Excise indicate the extent of illicit activity in Glenlivet and the surrounding area: no fewer than four hundred illicit stills were in operation in 1824. Not all the illicit stills at the time were concealed in caves and underground bunkers. Some hid in plain sight, like the distillery that operated undetected for many years in the clock tower in the very center of the whiskey town of Dufftown, a few miles from Glenlivet. The distillery was only discovered when the clock stopped and a passerby, who happened to be an excise officer, climbed the tower to investigate and found a still alongside the clock mechanism. Today the Dufftown Whisky Museum stands almost alongside the clock tower and has displays of some of the illicit stills from the area.

George Smith was not a full-time illicit whiskey maker but did a little on the side, just as his father before him had done. In fact, he trained as a carpenter and also worked on the family farm. Like many people of the time, he had several skills, all of which helped him to earn a living. An interesting man, he also studied Latin and architecture in his spare time, though they didn't provide much for the family coffers. Before passage of the 1823 act, he was said to be making about a hogshead of whiskey per week, which was probably about 50 gallons, or just under 200 liters. Although a sizable part-time operation, today the Glenlivet has seven stills, each capable of producing 10,000 liters of whiskey at a time.

Passage of the 1823 Excise Act immediately reversed the rapid decline in the numbers of legal distilleries. When the act was passed, there were 111 legal distilleries in Scotland. Two years later, there were 263. That decline of 26 percent turned, almost overnight, into an increase of 137 percent. Not only that, but the amount of whiskey produced legally tripled during the few years after the act. The Excise Act was so successful that within about ten years those illicit stills were no longer the threat to legal distilling that they had once been. The government even dared—no doubt while holding its breath—to gently raise excise duties again.

Incidentally, it was also fairly common for some of the whiskey produced in legal distilleries to find its way into the illicit market. Workers devised ingenious systems for smuggling spirit out of the distillery. One such device was known, not surprisingly, as a whiskey thief. Legitimate tools for workers in a distillery, these were tubes made of glass, wood, metal, or later plastic that were used like straws to draw whiskey from the barrel for sampling. Some workers adapted them so that they could be capped, slipped easily down their trouser leg, and taken home at the end of their shifts. The whiskey might be for personal use but in sufficient quantities could be bottled and sold on the black market.

Another way of stealing whiskey required advance planning. Builders who worked regularly on distillery construction would build a hidden hatch, usually in the roof, that allowed secret access to the distillery in the dead of night.

The success of the 1823 act presents a rosy picture for all but one group of people—the illicit distillers themselves. They were not a happy bunch. Illicit distilling had itself moved on from mainly disgruntled farmers who continued to defy the law to a moneymaking industry in its own right. Some illicit distillers made handsome profits, which they would not relinquish without a fight. The year that the act was passed, 1823, the Banks O'Dee Distillery was built in the Aberdeen area. Two years later, it was burned down by a gang of illicit distillers, their customers, and the smugglers who took their whiskeys to the markets beyond Aberdeenshire.

This was not the only legal distillery that was destroyed by the illicit traders, although they were definitely in retreat by this point. The island-based excise officers on Islay confiscated only five illicit stills from 1837 to 1843. However, records also stated that this was more to do with the laziness of those particular officers than with the lack of illegal activity.

Confiscating stills wasn't always a straightforward endeavor, either. One distiller in Perthshire had his equipment taken but found out where the excisemen were spending the night. The excisemen kept the equipment in their room, assuming that it (and they) was safe behind a locked door. The distiller had other ideas. He climbed in through a window and threw the excisemen's shoes out of the window. When the noise of his escape with his retrieved equipment woke the excisemen, they spent so long looking for their shoes in the room that he was able to show them, as it were, a clean pair of heels.

A resurgence in illicit distilling followed the passing of the Immature Spirits (Restriction) Act 1915. This legislation, which still applies today, requires that whiskey must be matured for at least three years before it can be legally sold as whiskey. Naturally this created a sudden scarcity of legal whiskey for the next three years, with the illicit distillers happy to fill the vacuum.

Then in 1920 two things happened that had illicit distillers rubbing their hands with glee once again and ramping up production. The first was that the British government—you guessed it—increased excise duties on whiskey. The second was even more momentous: the introduction of prohibition in the United States. This was to last for thirteen years, and during that time the demand for Scottish whiskey—both legal and illegal—went through the roof. Smuggling was rife, and the illicit distillers could hardly believe their luck. Not only was the British government helping increase demand for their product, but now the American government was joining in too.

The 1920s and 1930s were boom decades for illicit distilling in Scotland. One notable hotspot was the small town of Keith on Speyside, which today is a magnet for whiskey lovers. It's the starting point for the Scottish Malt Whisky Trail and the home of three distilleries: Strathmill, Glen Keith, and, most notably, Strathisla. Strathisla dates from 1786 and is one of the oldest continuously operating distilleries in Scotland.

Strathisla's long pedigree didn't stop one Keith hotelier from producing illicit whiskey almost on its doorstep. The Gordon Arms Hotel was on Mid Street, just a few minutes' walk from the distinguished distillery. On January 8, 1934, the hotel owner was charged in court with making spirits without a license in a cellar at the hotel.

The police had found a locked door in the cellar, which the owner claimed was merely a cupboard to which he had lost the key and they could ignore it. Not quite so easily deterred, the police forced the door and found a copper still, 15.7 gallons of spirit, eighteen packets of yeast, three bushels of malted barley, and all the other accoutrements that indicated a commercial distilling operation. The owner was fined £150 and the man who distributed his spirits as far as Aberdeen, about fifty miles away, was fined £50 (equivalent to around £13,200/$16,500 and £4,400/$5,500 respectively today).

Undeterred by the scale of such fines, Adam Riddoch, also from Keith, found himself in court three years later, also charged with illegal distilling. Excise officers had raided his home to find lengths of copper tubing, a sixty-gallon tank, and almost four hundred pounds of barley. Riddoch claimed that the tubing was for a wireless transmitter he was planning to make, the tank was for developing photographs (presumably very large ones), and the barley was to feed hens he was planning to buy. He was obviously a man with plans and he was acquitted, his case found "not proven," a verdict under Scottish law that means not necessarily innocent but without enough evidence to prove guilt.

It's always possible, of course, that the magistrate enjoyed a drop of the illegal stuff himself and was therefore inclined to turn a blind eye to suspicious activities. This was a problem the government faced repeatedly throughout the centuries in trying to enforce the law. Many of the people tasked with carrying out the laws were themselves buying or accepting gifts of illicit whiskey.

Even the clergy was often involved. Ministers of the church commonly received payment (in money or in kind) for blessing new stills that were about to go into production. They were then hardly likely to go running to the local exciseman and explain what they'd just done.

One minister, Alasdair Hutcheson, of Kiltarlity near Inverness, even turned his hand to smuggling to help boost his paltry income. Unfortunately, he upset one pub landlord, who thought Hutcheson was overcharging him, so he informed a local exciseman. The exciseman then embarked on an operation to catch Hutcheson with some illicit whiskey, which he did. The landlord, however, hadn't mentioned that Hutcheson was a minister, and the gauger was so surprised that he let the minister off with a warning not to do it again. He allowed Hutcheson to make another delivery to the landlord in question and then arrested the landlord for possession of illicit whiskey.

Excisemen themselves were often found to be involved in illicit distilling operations. Blind eyes were being turned everywhere.

Landowners were known to overlook illicit stills on their property and accept whiskey in lieu of rent.

One excise officer in Stornoway on the Isle of Lewis was given 15 shillings (75 pence/$1) by a particular smuggler for every cask of whiskey he turned a blind eye to. It was estimated that he tripled his annual salary due to his poor eyesight. Many others could be persuaded to develop impaired vision temporarily, including, in one memorable case, a prison guard.

Colin Macdonald recounts the story of the prison guard in his 1936 book, *Echoes of the Glen*. A distiller named John Macdonald operated two separate illicit distilleries around the Heights of Strathpeffer, northwest of Inverness in the Scottish Highlands. Macdonald was able to keep his operations totally secret until a gamekeeper walked through the roof of one of the underground distilleries while Macdonald was distilling:

> After trial, John was duly sentenced to be detained for a period of six weeks as an unwilling guest of His Majesty King William IV. John's wife walked to Dingwall every other day [a walk of almost two hours each way] bringing food for the prisoner. A fortnight went by without incident. Then John had a brain-wave. The old jailer was well-known to favour the cup that cheers; in fact he was possessed of a chronic and insatiable thirst—and on that John gambled—and won.
>
> During the remaining four weeks of the sentence there was observed a gentleman's agreement whereby every evening after dark John's cell door was unlocked. John then proceeded by a quiet route to the *Cnoc na Bainsse* bothy and there worked strenuously and in complete safety until returning dawn warned him it was time to make for his prison again; which he did—bringing with him in liquid form the price of the old jailer's complicity.
>
> As John's son put it to me, "The safest smuggling my father ever did was that time he was in Dingwall Jile."

Although not published till 1874, the book *Autobiography of Thomas Guthrie DD* describes a time in Guthrie's childhood prior to the passage of the 1823 Excise Act: "Everybody, with few exceptions, drank what was in reality illicit whiskey—far superior to that made under the eye of the Excise—lords and lairds, members of Parliament and ministers of the gospel."

This was as true in the 1920s as it was in the 1820s, and as true in the United States during Prohibition as it had been in Scotland. Although Prohibition came to an end in 1933, Scotland's illicit spirits trade continued to flourish. Just before World War II, one still was discovered in the town of Wick in northeast Scotland, less than a hundred yards from the Old Pulteney Distillery. Then when World War II broke out in 1939, it led to a huge black market in many things that became hard to buy legally. Whiskey was one of those items, and the illicit stills continued in full production.

In Glasgow in the 1960s, an illegal distilling operation was discovered on Gallowgate. The distiller used a washing machine as a mash tun, mixing the ground malt with water at the right temperature, the process prior to distilling and also used in brewing.

And still they continue today, although these days, illicit stills are more likely to be housed in factories than on farms and just as likely to produce vodka and other spirits as whiskey. In December 2021, a police raid on an industrial unit in Greenock, about twenty-five miles west of Glasgow, found 425 liters of counterfeit vodka in an illegal distillery. There were also two stills and several pallets of empty bottles waiting to be filled, along with containers holding around 12,000 liters of industrial spirit.

Joe Hendry, assistant director of the fraud investigation service at HMRC (His Majesty's Revenue and Customs), said at the time: "HMRC and our partners will not tolerate the sale of illegal alcohol. Drinking counterfeit alcohol can be a huge risk to health and even cause death. Disrupting criminal trade is at the heart of our strategy to clamp down on the illicit alcohol market which costs the UK around £1 billion per year. This is theft from the taxpayer and undermines legitimate traders."

At least the illicit distillers of old were primarily local people making real whiskey as they had done for generations. Today's illicit distillers are more likely to be organized gangs producing fake products of dubious quality that are possibly harmful to health. This kind of criminal activity happens all over the world, of course, and not just in Scotland, though in the next chapter we see that Scotland also had a role to play in the international smuggling trade.

DANGERS OF ILLICIT ALCOHOL

1. Toxic contaminants: Illicit alcohol may contain harmful contaminants, such as methanol (wood alcohol), acetone, ethyl acetate, or other toxic chemicals. Methanol, in particular, can cause severe poisoning and lead to symptoms such as nausea, vomiting, abdominal pain, blindness, coma, and even death.

2. Poorly regulated production: Illicit alcohol is often produced in unlicensed or clandestine facilities where production methods may not adhere to safety standards. This can result in the presence of harmful substances or impurities in the final product.

3. Unsafe ingredients: Illicit alcohol producers may use cheap or inappropriate ingredients in their production process, such as industrial-grade alcohol or denatured alcohol, which can be harmful when consumed.

4. High alcohol content: Illicit alcohol may have higher alcohol content than regulated alcoholic beverages, increasing the risk of alcohol poisoning and overdose.

5. Adulteration: Illicit alcohol may be adulterated with other substances, such as diluents, flavorings, or colorants, which can be harmful to health.

6. Lack of quality control: Illicit alcohol production lacks the quality control measures implemented in licensed and regulated distilleries, increasing the likelihood of contamination or impurities in the final product.

7. Risk of methanol poisoning: Illicitly produced spirits are at a higher risk of containing dangerous levels of methanol, which can occur due to improper distillation techniques or the addition of methanol-containing substances to increase potency. Methanol poisoning can cause severe health effects, including blindness and death.

· 2 ·

SMUGGLING

23rd February [1924]—Discovered some new combinations
on the concertina this evening. Quite well pleased with myself.
—ALASTAIR MORAY, *THE DIARY OF A RUM-RUNNER*

The life of a smuggler isn't all about dodging bullets and the Coast
Guard. In his entertaining book *The Diary of a Rum-Runner* (1929),
Alastair Moray describes a life that's a mixture of danger and tedium, in
which smugglers are more likely to be dodging storms and the captain's
temper or finding ways to amuse themselves. A couple of weeks before
the entry that starts this chapter, Moray wrote: "I have made a Japanese
violin out of a cigar-box." Then the next day: "Spent a busy day making
a set of chessmen out of the wood pillars round the back of the settee,
the kings and queens from the knobs on the ends of the curtain rods,
the knights out of a board off a whiskey-case."

A few days later he records the real purpose of his voyage: "I am
getting quite a collection of dollar bills—about twenty-two thousand
at present. I should like to go ashore when I have forty thousand and
get rid of it!"

One month later: "Checked all my money. I have $65,845 to hand
into the bank tomorrow."

It was a lucrative trip. Moray began the journey in September 1923,
and by March 1924, he was about to bank the equivalent of $1.2 mil-
lion in today's money—and that wasn't his only bank visit during the
voyage.

It's worth looking at Moray's book in some detail—and indeed reading in full if you can get a copy—as it reveals a lot about the realities of a smuggler's life. Despite the title, which uses the term "rum-runner" as a generic name for a smuggler, Moray was part of a crew that spent eleven months at sea, taking a cargo of mainly illicit whiskey along with gin, wine, and other booze from his native Scotland to the Caribbean and then to the eastern coast of the United States, taking full advantage of the demands for drink in the United States created by Prohibition.

Moray's adventure began near the Central Station in Glasgow, where he bumped into a friend who asked him, "How would you like to go as supercargo in a rum-runner?" The supercargo is the crew member responsible for overseeing the cargo and its eventual sale. Moray met the man organizing the trip, who told him about plans to take about 20,000 cases of whiskey to the US coast on a voyage lasting three to four months. If successful, he planned two more voyages later.

We learn nothing of Moray's background, his job, or his family. Presumably he is single and not unfamiliar with illegal activities, since

THE VOLSTEAD ACT

The Volstead Act, officially known as the National Prohibition Act, was enacted by US Congress in 1919 to enforce the Eighteenth Amendment to the Constitution, which prohibited the manufacture, sale, and transportation of alcoholic beverages. The wording of the Volstead Act included provisions for the enforcement of Prohibition, defining what constituted intoxicating liquor and outlining penalties for violations. Here's the principal text of the Volstead Act: "An Act to prohibit intoxicating beverages, and to regulate the manufacture, production, use, and sale of high-proof spirits for other than beverage purposes, and to insure an ample supply of alcohol and promote its use in scientific research and in the development of fuel, dye, and other lawful industries."

he expresses no surprise at being asked to smuggle whiskey into the United States. In fact, he accepts the job offer the next day and sets out to equip himself: "I was informed that an unarmed ship out there was as safe as the proverbial snowflake, so, with the object of being safer than the snowflake, I purchased six .450 Webley revolvers, one Colt .450, an automatic .38, and plenty of ammunition."

Moray clearly knew where to buy his arsenal, and next he buys a safe in which to stash the proceeds of his endeavors. He's soon overseeing the loading of the cargo, and despite guarding against theft, he sees some members of the loading crew getting steadily drunk. After all, it takes a long time to manually load 20,000 cases, and he can't be everywhere at once. One man was stopped as he tried to walk off with eleven cases of whiskey on a handcart. As we see later in this book, loading and unloading crews are skilled at hiding cargo and helping themselves to it in all manner of ways.

The journey begins with the four-masted schooner, *Cask*—an appropriate name, though the ship has definitely seen better days—sailing down the River Clyde. Rather than heading west across the Atlantic, the ship first heads south, along the coast of Britain, to the port of Le Havre on the north coast of France.

This is a procedure common among smugglers. Before leaving Glasgow, the ship's owner would have to make a payment to the Customs and Excise office, which was refundable when the goods were unloaded at their destination. Because the goods would be sold illegally, piecemeal, to whomever turned up to buy them, the owner risked losing his customs payment. The way around this was to unload them officially at a convenient port, get an unloading certificate, and send it back to the ship's owner to enable him to claim his refund. The goods were then loaded back on board, out of sight of any officials, and the ship made its way to where it intended to go all along.

Meanwhile, in Cuba, a similar procedure happened over and over again to enable goods to be smuggled to the United States, as we read later in this chapter. Here the cargo was rum, which would be loaded in one Cuban port, unloaded in another Cuban port, where it would ostensibly be legally exported, perhaps to Europe, only to be reloaded and head to the United States illegally. In other cases, unloading certificates were forged or bought from bribable officials. Not all of the cargo from Moray's ship found its way back on board, instead ending up inside many of the two hundred Frenchmen who were unloading and re-loading at Le Havre.

After the bureaucratic sleight of hand, Moray's book describes the very real dangers of taking an older ship on a voyage across the Atlantic. One problem is that there isn't much room for the storage of fresh food and drink supplies, so the ship has to load up whenever it has the op-portunity. Bad weather frequently drives the ship off course. Equipment breaks and isn't always repairable onboard, requiring additional stops. And crew members sometimes have had enough and jump ship or are fired and left to fend for themselves in the next port of call, leaving the ship short of crew when no replacements can be found. Occasionally stowaways are discovered and, if they have any skills at all, might be recruited as crew members. If not, they are thrown off at the next port.

Eventually *Cask* somehow makes it to Bermuda, and the crew get busy selling what they can of the cargo before heading north to the United States. Moray's entry for December 20 records sales of more than a thousand cases of whiskey in five hours, and at the end of the day he counts $31,760 in his safe. All transactions were made in cash, in US dollars, so Moray is responsible for what would be almost $600,000 in today's money. If your image of smugglers were of illiterate and unskilled thugs who couldn't get better jobs, think again. Moray proves to be a witty and observant writer, a versatile musician, and a more-than-competent businessman.

Eventually *Cask* makes it to the coast off New York, where it's moored on Rum Row. During Prohibition, it was illegal to make and sell alcohol in the United States. The US government pressured other countries, notably Cuba, to help them enforce the laws outside the United States; unsurprisingly, this wasn't very successful. Too much money was being made, both legally and illegally, for countries to sup-press the sale of alcohol within their own borders simply to show sol-idarity with a law that wasn't even popular in the United States itself.

Accordingly, the rule against selling alcohol was enforceable only within the borders of the United States, which included US territo-rial waters that extended—according to Moray—twelve miles (19 km) offshore. Therefore it was not illegal for a boat to moor itself, say, thirteen miles (21 km) offshore and sell the alcohol on board. Neither was it illegal for US citizens to visit that boat and buy alcohol. For some reason, Prohibition did not ban the buying of alcohol (nor the drinking of it), only the making, transportation, and selling of it. The crime was committed as soon as the US citizen transported the alcohol within US territorial waters. The aim, therefore, was not to get caught.

In fact, it was generally accepted that legal jurisdiction anywhere extended only three miles (4.8 km) offshore, but during Prohibition, the United States lobbied to extend this to twelve miles. Although never legally enforceable, many countries accepted the new boundaries in a gentleman's agreement. This led to confusion in the American courts of law: many smugglers were acquitted because although they were caught within the twelve-mile limit, they were outside the three-mile zone, and their lawyers argued successfully that they were acting within the law.

Avoiding getting caught in the first place wasn't difficult, since the US coastline extended about 18,000 miles (29,000 km) and the United States didn't have nearly enough Coast Guard officers to police it. Even if they concentrated on the busiest areas, like Florida and the coast near New York, the Coast Guard couldn't watch every mile. Even in one of the busiest areas, the 500 miles (805 km) of coast between St. Augustine and Key West in Florida, there were only five customs officers. One Coast Guard officer described the task facing them as going lion hunting with a peashooter. Even by 1932, twelve years after the start of Prohibition, the Coast Guard had only two patrol boats to police the waters between New York City and Fort Lauderdale, a distance of more than 1,000 miles (1,610 km).

So it was easy for *Cask* and all the other rum-running vessels to drop anchor just beyond the twelve-mile limit and form little communities that became known as Rum Row. On one occasion, the crew of the *Cask* discovered that they had drifted only eleven-and-a-half miles offshore, so they hurried back to legal safety.

Even when the authorities discovered that smugglers were there, they stood little chance of apprehending the offending US boats that visited Rum Row at all hours of the day and night. The rum-runners could simply hang out there in international waters till they sold out, coming ashore from time to time to buy food or get their equipment repaired. They could then bank the profits, sail off to restock, and do the same thing all over again. It was, for the most part, a pleasant way for the rum-runners to pass the time. Typical Moray diary entries describe life on board while waiting for customers to show up:

> Played Cheery four games of chess, and won three. I haven't had time yet to make pawns, so we used instead revolver cartridges. . . . Practised my concertina for a bit, and finished the chessmen. . . . During the afternoon the mate suggested I should compose a Bootleggers' March for the pipes [Moray also played the bagpipes], so in the evening I sought inspiration and have got something down on paper. . . . Tried over my *March to Rum Row* for the pipes; with a few alterations it will not be bad—at least, that is the composer's opinion.

It wasn't all chess and concertinas, though. The crew was on constant watch to protect their valuable cargo and cash from modern-day pirates and even other rum-runners. A rum-running ship is an obvious target for thieves. The ship wouldn't be there if it wasn't well stocked with drink that fetched high prices or with at least some of the proceeds from selling it. Not every operation bothered to use banks. One notorious smuggling ring in Mobile, Alabama, used checks drawn on the People's Bank of Mobile rather than risk large amounts of cash. The bank's president was, conveniently, a member of the smuggling ring.

A typical price for a case of whiskey, Moray records, was about $17—about $300 in today's currency—though it depended on the quality and the quantity bought. Inevitably some bargaining occurred, especially if trade was slow and they wanted to shift stock. With that much cash as well as thousands of cases of hooch, the rewards for bandits robbing these ships were akin to raiding Fort Knox. Bootleggers might also attack the ship and simply take the whiskey to resell themselves. Moray gives accounts of other boats being attacked and their cargo sold at half price to other rum-runners, who could then mark it up and make a profit while undercutting the other boats—including the one that had been robbed. There was certainly no honor among thieves when it came to smuggling. "One boat about five miles east of us was raided not long ago. One partner was on board as supercargo, the other doing the shore end. The shore end lad had a raid carried out and cleared off after with, I am told, about $40,000."

A few months after this incident, Moray writes:

I have had a lot of warnings against piracy and shall have to be on the watch. One boat was caught in the narrows, a fifty-foot boat with twenty men on her, twenty-two rifles, twenty automatic pistols, and sixteen pairs of handcuffs. That wasn't there for nothing. . . . We have mapped out a golf course on the poop. . . . At present I hold the Championship with a score of twenty-five for nine holes.

Moray and his colleagues were never raided, partly because they were a sizable crew themselves, well-armed, and watchful. On a few occasions they were approached by other ships that seemed to be checking them out and up to no good, but the would-be robbers thought better of raiding when they saw how well-defended the *Cask* was. When they're not watching for bandits, life on board goes on: "Cheery and the mate engaged in a fierce argument as to whether all gooseberries have hair or not, and nearly came to blows over it."

On July 14, 1924, Moray describes a good day's trading, with 950 cases of whiskey sold, but the following day, he realizes it wasn't as profitable as he'd thought: "When I counted over the money again by daylight some of the fifty-dollar bills looked funny, and, now that I have compared them with others I have, I am afraid they are spurious— seven hundred dollars' worth."

He soon discovers that he got off lightly, as the captain of another ship took $11,000 in fake notes and shot himself because of it. In all, $90,000 in counterfeit currency was used, and Moray finds that $50 notes are selling for $15 onshore. For all its risks, Moray clearly enjoyed his life at sea, though we never learn how much money he personally made from what turned into almost a year away. One of his later entries, when the ship was back in Bermuda prior to returning to Scotland, reads: "1st August. Beautiful morning. Went through a school of about seventeen whales. They are diving under the ship."

At the same time that Moray was helping to satisfy whiskey lovers in the United States during Prohibition, Cuban smugglers were catering to rum drinkers. In fact, much of the liquor that made its way illegally into the United States came from or via Cuba, a story that is thoroughly told in the book *A Thousand Thirsty Beaches: Smuggling Alcohol from Cuba to the South during Prohibition* (2018) by Lisa Lindquist Dorr.

As in Scotland, deceitful documents played a prominent role in Cuba. Dorr gives one such example in her introduction. A boat found itself in trouble off the Louisiana coast, and a Coast Guard cutter arrived to help. A Coast Guard officer was the last person the ship's captain wanted to see. He insisted his ship needed no help, which raised the officer's suspicions, because it clearly did.

Reviewing the cargo manifest, the officer saw that the ship was allegedly heading from Havana to Honduras with more than three thousand cases of liquor on board. So what was it doing off the coast of Louisiana with only seven hundred cases? The weather could not have blown it off its course to Honduras, more than a thousand miles (1,609 km) south of Louisiana. On this occasion, it seemed like a victory for the law over the lawbreakers. However, the case was dismissed in court and the ship and its contents returned to the captain. It doesn't take a genius to work out what he would have done with it.

As long as you weren't among the people who regarded smuggling as a problem, the case of Cuban exports of booze to Honduras was quite amusing. The paperwork shows that between 1919 and 1924, exports of liquor from Cuba to Honduras increased by more than 726,796 gallons. Most of these supposedly went through the port of Limón. However, there was no customs officer there who was qualified to certify the required clearance documents. Nor was there much evidence of any liquor actually arriving at the port for distribution. Of more than $500,000 of liquor that allegedly left Havana for various Honduran ports, only $1,822 worth could be documented to have actually arrived.

Dorr describes how ships full of liquor were arriving in New York from Cuba within two months of the enactment of Prohibition on January 16, 1920. In fact, plans for smuggling were being prepared

PIRATES OF THE CARIBBEAN

In this chapter we look at what happened in the Caribbean during Prohibition, but what happened during the swashbuckling days at the heights of piracy? Come to think of it, what is swashbuckling anyway? Are you swashing a buckle or buckling a swash? In fact, the word comes from "buckler," which is a kind of small shield, and "swashing," which means prancing around with sword drawn. Pirates tended not to bother with bucklers, since they needed one hand free to hold onto the rigging—or possibly their opponent's neck—but when they were going about their piratical deeds, they would definitely hold a sword, a pistol, a musket, or even a grenade in the other hand.

So were pirates involved in liquor crimes? Of course they were. They drank mostly rum, and stealing it was cheaper than buying it. They plundered ships for whatever they could take to sell or to trade or to consume themselves. Many pirate ships were in fact privateers; privateers acted on behalf of a government, attacking the ships of its enemies, whereas pirates were the equivalent of today's self-employed worker.

Pirate ships have existed for most of history and in most places around the world; notorious spots include the Straits of Malacca in Malaysia, the Straits of Gibraltar between the Mediterranean and the Atlantic, off the coast of Africa, and in the Caribbean. The Caribbean became a focus because European nations such as Great Britain, France, and Spain all established colonies there, so there were rich pickings to be had from ships laden with goods being traded and carrying large amounts of money. In the Caribbean there was also, naturally, a great deal of rum.

Some ships carried nothing but rum, and the pirates would help themselves to the barrels and go off on benders, rendering further piracy impossible for a while. Incidentally, pirates never said or sang, "Yo-ho-ho and a bottle of rum." It was a phrase invented by the author Robert Louis Stevenson for his book about pirates, *Treasure Island*.

even before Prohibition became law. Once it was, an immediate, steady stream of boats made use of that southern US coastline, which was ideal for smuggling: thinly populated with plenty of inlets, waterways, and beaches. Many Southerners disapproved of Prohibition, having long enjoyed a taste for regular "libations," so there was a keen local market for the booze. It was also close to Cuba and other Caribbean islands, which would become hotbeds of smuggling.

It was easy and legal, for example, for the British to suddenly start exporting vast amounts of Scotch whiskey to its own colony of the Bahamas. What happened to it after it reached the Bahamas was none of their concern, as long as they were paid for it. What if the good citizens of the Bahamas suddenly and unexpectedly developed a huge taste for Johnnie Walker? So what if more cases of whiskey were sent to the Bahamas than the island's entire population could drink in a lifetime? *Nothing to do with us*, the governments of countries including Great Britain and Canada told an increasingly frustrated US government.

In fact, Canada made sure it profited from the US demand for drink. It imposed a duty of $20 on every case exported to the United States. Of course, that was only the legal exports. And in Cuba, members of the government themselves owned distilleries whose profits were being boosted thanks to Prohibition. They were known to work with the smuggling rings thus were unlikely to help the United States enforce an internal law externally. And it wasn't just about distillery profits. The Cuban government collected export duties on the estimated $80 million per year of alcohol that was passing through the country. In addition, Havana was a huge port where the ships bought provisions and paid for repairs and their crews spent their money between trips.

The increase in liquor smuggling was soon joined by increased illegal importation of other products, like tobacco, and then the importation of people. Those who could not enter the United States legally could book passage on a rum-runner and be dropped off in the United States along with the cases of rum. They were also smuggled in along the land borders, accompanying consignments of Canadian whiskey and Mexican tequila. The immigrants were happy, and the rum-runners were happy and even richer, because they were also using the immigrants as unpaid labor to load and unload the liquor. Foreign governments were happy to boost their export trade. Only the US government was ticked off, and it expected other countries to help enforce US laws. Its disappointment isn't surprising.

By 1924, an estimated 100,000 cases of liquor were arriving illegally on southern and eastern US coasts *every month*, with only about 5 percent being intercepted. Add to that the long land borders with both Mexico and Canada, and the scale of the operations becomes obvious. As the *New York Times* observed in October 1921: "It would take all the navies in the world to successfully block" the importation of liquor. Dorr observes: "That Americans would continue to want to drink alcohol even without the organized efforts of the liquor industry to promote it took dry advocates entirely by surprise." Indeed, the proponents of Prohibition seemed to think that by making alcohol sales illegal, people would soon change their habits and no longer bother with drinking. But more of that in chapter 4.

Miami was one place that refused to change its habits. Its economy depended on its reputation as a leading winter resort where visitors from elsewhere in the United States could go for both sunshine and a good time—which for many people included a drink. Hotel owners and others, including politicians, did not like Prohibition being forced upon them by the federal government. Their response was to act as if the law had never been passed. Bootleggers openly advertised their current stock of liquor in the *Miami Life* newspaper. Smuggling activity increased enormously whenever a convention came to town, especially political ones. This led to conflict and even murder.

In one case the Coast Guard chased a high-speed smuggling vessel, which headed into the canals of the city itself. The Coast Guard shot and killed one bootlegger in full view of guests at the Fleetwood Hotel, where witnesses said that the bootlegger had his hands in the air in surrender and was no threat to the Coast Guard. Five of the Coast Guard were charged with murder.

On the lighter side, an entertaining section of *A Thousand Thirsty Beaches* tells the story of "Uncle Sam's Booze Cops," a group of civilians in Havana recruited by the US government to spy on and undermine the smuggling operations in the city. On occasion, it was more like the Keystone Cops. One member of the group, Salvador Pena, got a job as ship's engineer on a smuggling vessel. He found forged papers on board that said that the current cargo had already been unloaded in Honduras, though the dates were blank.

The ship instead headed for Alabama, and Pena figured out that if they encountered the Coast Guard, he could cause the ship's engine to malfunction by spitting on it, enabling the Coast Guard's inferior vessel to catch them. When the time came, he worried that spitting would be insufficient, so he urinated on the carburetor. This worked, the Coast Guard came aboard, investigated, and arrested the crew. Yet again, however, the charges were dismissed, and the ship and its illicit cargo were handed back to the captain. No one knows why so many smuggling cases were dismissed. It may have been due to legal technicalities, or it may have been because there was so much collusion and corruption going on. Or perhaps some of the judges enjoyed a drink, opposed Prohibition, and decided not to enforce it.

Pena's cover was never blown, and he continued to infiltrate the smuggling networks. He also exposed the trade in forged paperwork by the simple method of buying some forgeries himself, and he and his colleagues in "Uncle Sam's Booze Cops" (which is how they referred to themselves) were more effective in curtailing Cuban smuggling than the politicians had ever been. And although the "cops" may have been working fully in support of Prohibition, it didn't stop them from enthusiastically enjoying their Cuban rum.

———•—•———

Earlier in this chapter, we read about the large amounts of whiskey and other spirits being smuggled out of Great Britain, especially Scotland, in the early twentieth century, mainly to satisfy the thirsts of people living with Prohibition in the United States. However, there has always been a flourishing trade smuggling liquor *into* Great Britain over the years. As we saw in chapter 1, British governments have always been fond of slapping taxes on alcohol, not for puritanical reasons, but initially to raise money to fund armies for a succession of wars.

And old habits die hard. As of this writing, 39 percent of a £10 bottle of wine sold in the United Kingdom goes to the government by way of excise duties and VAT (value added tax). The VAT is levied on the duty payable, so in the United Kingdom, even the tax is taxed when you're buying booze! And that's only on still wine below 15 percent alcohol by volume (ABV). For sparkling wines and wines that are 15 percent ABV and higher, the government rakes in even more money. When you allow for the cost of the bottle, the label, the bottling, the shipping (maybe from as far as Australia), and the store's markup, the actual wine in the bottle is worth only a few pounds, and somewhere along the way the winemaker has to scrape a profit too. Suffice it to say that in Britain the government makes more on alcohol sales than the producers do, so little wonder that smuggling has always been a popular occupation.

And not just smuggling alcohol, either. The British love of tea is reflected in the smuggling statistics. It's estimated that in the eighteenth century, only 20 percent of all the tea drunk in England had gone through the official channels and had duty paid on it. At that time, about 70 percent of the cost of tea was due to taxation, so you could hardly blame the average person for looking for a cheaper cup of char and for colluding with the smugglers who provided those options.

In many cases, those smugglers were family and friends, and were as likely to be Cornish fishermen setting off for France as French fishermen sailing for England. Sometimes the rewards of smuggling were so good that they no longer bothered fishing, or they switched between the two according to circumstances. In British ports, which naturally attracted the smuggling trade, it was common to find French and Dutch fishermen and sailors in the taverns at night, spending some of their takings and drumming up orders for their next crossing.

The British writer Daniel Defoe included a visit to the Kent town of Faversham in his 1825 book, *Tour through the Whole Island of Great Britain*: "I know nothing else this town is remarkable for, except the most notorious smuggling trade, carried on partly by the assistance of the Dutch, in their oyster boats. . . . The people hereabouts are arrived to such proficiency that they are grown monstrous rich by that wicked trade."

In the same book, Defoe visits Southampton, 120 miles from Faversham on the south coast, and there also notes: "Southampton is a truly antient [*sic*] town, for 'tis in a manner dying with age; the decay of the trade is the real decay of the town; and all the business of moment that is transacted there, is the trade between us and the islands of Jersey and Guernsey, with a little of the wine trade, and much smuggling."

Perhaps Defoe referred to smuggling as a "wicked trade" because he was himself a legitimate merchant, dealing in wine and trading in Cadiz in Spain and Porto and Lisbon in Portugal. He also worked for the government and, as well as being a suspected spy, was responsible for collecting the taxes on bottles. (Yes, the bottles themselves were also taxed, not just what went into them.)

A hundred years before Defoe, Bristol merchants were also trading with Spain, importing and exporting various goods. Imports naturally included Spanish wines, and exports included cannons, which Britain happened to be good at making. So it turned out that when the Spanish decided to try to invade England in 1588 and sent out their *felicissima*

THE SPANISH ARMADA

The Spanish Armada was a fleet of ships sent by King Philip II of Spain in 1588 to invade England and overthrow Queen Elizabeth I. It was a response to England's support for Protestant rebels in the Spanish-ruled Netherlands and the raids of English privateers on Spanish ships. The Armada consisted of around 130 ships and more than twenty thousand men, including soldiers and sailors. However, it faced a series of setbacks, including bad weather and English naval tactics led by Sir Francis Drake and others. The English successfully repelled the invasion in what became known as the Battle of Gravelines, and the remnants of the Armada were forced to sail around Scotland and Ireland, where they were further decimated by storms.

armada, or "most fortunate fleet," the 130 or so ships were armed with cannons made in England. Just as today, few governments or private companies saw anything wrong in trading with the enemy if there was money to be made.

━━━━◆━━━━

Although smuggling was rife in certain places in the United Kingdom, including the rugged shores of Cornwall in the southwest and the county of Kent in the southeast, smuggling took place around almost the entire coast of the British Isles. One small boat could cross the English Channel from France in a few hours, carrying up to three thousand gallons of wine or spirits.

Kent could be regarded as the birthplace of smuggling in England, although initially it was for exports, not imports. Nicknamed the "Garden of England" for its wealth of orchards and hop fields, Kent's proximity to both London and to northern Europe made it an ideal place for a spot of illegal activity. This goes back to at least the thirteenth century, when exports of wool from England began to be taxed, making it much more profitable to export wool illegally.

Wool was the first item on which export duties were levied in 1275, and at the same time, naturally, the first people were appointed as customs officers responsible for collecting the money.

One person who tried his hand at wool smuggling was a Cistercian monk named Abbot Robert. We'll soon see that the church and smuggling were always closely connected. Back in 1423 it was recorded that Abbot Robert, who was head of Furness Abbey in Cumbria, northwest England, was smuggling wool to Zealand in Denmark on a one-hundred-ton ship. The fells around the abbey and around Cumbria generally have always been good sheep country. And it's not surprising that the abbey was involved in smuggling; at one time the abbey, which had been founded in 1123, was the second wealthiest and most powerful abbey in England after Fountains Abbey in Yorkshire. Positions of power and wealth had to be maintained, and there's no commandment that says "Thou shalt not smuggle."

The kind of profits to be made from unlawful trading of this kind are indicated by the illegal activities of the legal-sounding Seasalter Company. This company was founded in the isolated little community of Seasalter, near Whitstable on the North Kent coast. The very isolation of the place helped turn it into a busy smuggling center, and the Seasalter Company made the most of it by bringing in spirits and other goods from continental Europe and transporting them to London, slightly more than fifty miles (80 km) away. The company was founded in 1740; in 1812, when William Baldock, one of its partners, died, his will revealed an estate worth more than £1 million (today's value would be approximately £87 million, or $110 million). And Baldock was only one of the partners.

From the government's point of view, a big part of the smuggling problem—as we saw in chapter 1—was that everyone was involved. The customer was as likely to be the local vicar buying sherry and tea as the lord of the manor purchasing port, wine, and brandy. The lord of the manor also might have originally put up the money to fund the operation and pay for the smuggled goods, whereas a local farmer may have loaned the smugglers his horses to carry the cases and barrels in return for part of the consignment.

The rector of the Suffolk village of Great Bealings, near Ipswich, was kind enough to leave his stables unlocked whenever he knew that the local smugglers were in need of horses. He even let them use his carriage to transport booze, reasoning that anyone who knew about the arrangement didn't care, and anyone who didn't know would assume the rector's carriage was taken without his knowledge.

In Glen Isla in Scotland, the Reverend Andrew Burns happened to live overlooking the hotel where visiting excisemen stayed. He watched for them, perhaps tipped off by the hotel owner, and as soon as they arrived, he rode around warning the local distillers. Smugglers commonly made arrangements with local vicars to use their churches as safe storage places for contraband. Gin might be stored in the church tower, or whiskey stashed under the pulpit.

Pubs were also common hiding places for illegal liquor, whether the landlord was buying it or merely storing it. They seldom used their own cellars, which would have been natural targets for customs officers, but would use secret cellars or rooms. One pub, the Spread Eagle in the Essex town of Witham, had a clever arrangement. Look at the building today (now called the AKA Restaurant), and you can see its tall chimneys. One of these was no longer operational—not as a chimney, anyway. The only access was from the roof. Smugglers lowered their goods down the chimney at night, where they would be safe from prying eyes.

Other places of concealment included pits dug in the sand dunes behind beaches used by smugglers. This could involve a lot of work, especially to hide footsteps and signs of construction in the sand. The pits had to be solid sand for at least 6 feet, as that was the length of the poles that customs officers used to probe the sand searching for pits. However, once built, such pits provided useful hiding places close at hand when cargoes were unloaded, which could be collected later when no one was around and there wasn't the pressure of unloading cargo and dispersing it quickly.

The sea was also used to hide smuggled goods. Instead of bringing them to shore, boats dropped goods over the side, weighed down with heavy objects. Sometimes barrels were tied to planks that were designed to float above the barrel but below the surface of the sea at low tide, making them easier to locate for recovery. Sometimes floats for lobster pots actually marked the locations of barrels on the seabed.

Caves were used, and village ponds also provided convenient temporary hiding places. One clever method was to use places or rooms that were allegedly haunted, which discouraged people from investigating too closely. Obviously the smugglers were happy to spread or embellish the stories of hauntings—the more gruesome and scary, the better.

For James Woodforde, the parson in the Norfolk village of Weston Longville, near Norwich, smuggling was such an everyday part of life that he even recorded it in his diary. He wrote about buying gin, brandy, and tea from various people. The blacksmith in the village of Honingham, about four miles from Weston Longville, was even referred to as Robert "Moonshine" Buck. He clearly kept more in his workshop than hammers and an anvil.

Woodforde also recorded the following incident, showing that his wife was fully aware of what was happening: "Andrews the smuggler brought me this night about 11 o'clock a bag of Hyson Tea 6 Pd weight. He frightened us a little by whistling under the parlour window just as we were going to bed. I gave him some Geneva and paid for the tea at 10/6 a Pd." Geneva refers to genever, the Dutch style of gin, showing that Woodforde was a spiritual man indeed.

Almost everyone was involved in smuggling. Indeed, in 1770 even the mayor of Penzance, John Tonkin, was convicted of smuggling while in office. What was unusual about this case was that he was actually charged in the first place. In many towns and cities, anyone with influential friends would get away with smuggling, as they were all involved in one way or another. This wasn't an isolated case. In 1767 John Knill was the mayor of St. Ives, another Cornish coastal town, and the collector of customs. He was also a smuggler.

An incident in the town of Conwy in North Wales demonstrates the state of things. A smuggled load of salt was taken to the beach by boat, and half the town turned out to help unload and transport it. Leading the procession of salt-filled carts was a distinguished knight of the realm and local justice of the peace (JP), Sir Griffith Williams. There was no peace for the solitary customs officer who had turned up to do his job; when he saw the people, he decided that discretion was the better part of valor and tried to hide instead. Unfortunately for him, he was spotted, and some of the townspeople beat him and kept him prisoner in a hen-house for a day, till the salt was safely disposed of. When he was released, the customs officer reported the incident to the police, but naturally nothing came of it due to the high status of some of those involved.

Salt wasn't the only seasoning traded by smugglers. At one point, the tax on pepper was so high that it became a profitable item to smuggle. Smugglers in Cornwall began to specialize in it, so much so that their favorite landing place near the town of Porthcothan became known as Pepper Cove. These landing places weren't chosen at random. Smugglers preferred sandy beaches that shelved gently, enabling bigger boats to be hauled ashore. Isolation helped, of course, as did high cliffs to conceal activity, but a quick escape route was also required in order to remove the goods as swiftly as possible.

Candles, or the tallow wax to make candles, were also a desirable smuggling item. It seems that over the years successive governments didn't want people to eat, drink, or see in the dark without ensuring their cut. In the coastal village of Solva in Pembrokeshire, Wales, even the Baptist Chapel was lit by candles made from smuggled tallow wax. When the local excise officer heard about this, he raided an evening service and confiscated all the candles, leaving the congregation to pray in the dark.

Other smuggled items were revealed in the records kept by the customs house in Aberdeen. In just one month, November 1721, they recorded more than one thousand gallons of brandy, 3,059 pounds of tobacco (1,388 kg), casks containing prunes, currants, raisins, figs, soap, starch, aniseed, molasses, and licorice, as well as quantities of writing paper, twine, and bars of iron from Sweden.

Back in North Wales, another JP, William Bulkeley of Anglesey, was also happy to buy smuggled goods, as he recorded in his diaries. The island of Anglesey, off the coast of North Wales, was a hotbed of smuggling. Bulkeley bought white wine, claret, and brandy from a smuggler who was bringing goods from the Isle of Man, about forty-five miles (72 km) north of Anglesey in the middle of the Irish Sea, where taxes were much lower. In Britain, one of a JP's responsibilities is administering the law, and Bulkeley always tried to dismiss charges against smugglers if he thought he could get away with it.

This network of involvement in smuggling sometimes extended to funding smuggling operations. Unless some bartering was going on, there could be considerable amounts of cash to be found to fund an operation. Often a wealthy landowner would put up the money, or local people could band together in a kind of smuggling cooperative. Everyone involved would put in the same amount and recoup it when the goods were sold, or people might chip in differing amounts according to what they wanted and the smuggled goods were, in effect, presold.

Such a setup meant that it was in everyone's interest that no one in authority should hear about what was going on. This arrangement also spread the risk, so that if anything went wrong—like a boat being intercepted or losing its cargo in a storm—no single individual was financially ruined. It was possible, though, to insure against such things with Lloyd's of London, so much a part of everyday life were smuggling activities. In 1798 in the town of Amlwch on the north coast of

Anglesey, about as close to the smuggling sources on the Isle of Man as you could get, fourteen people chipped in to buy their own boat. These included the local doctor and a customs house officer, which must have been useful.

Around this time, the Shetland Islands in Scotland experienced a cash shortage due to the amount of money spent buying smuggled gin. However, it should be remembered that the use of cash was very different back then. Many people had very little actual cash, relying more on self-sufficiency and barter. Even rent agreements might stipulate that the rent was payable in corn, meat, fish, or, of course, whiskey. Bank of England bank notes had been in existence for only a hundred years at that time, being introduced in 1694, when the Bank of England was established. That was also when private individuals—well, anyone who had some cash to spare—could open private bank accounts. For long periods, only notes in large denominations were available, the likes of which average people would never see in their lifetime. If they splurged on illicit gin or whiskey—perhaps in the hope of making a small profit by reselling it—people couldn't simply go to the ATM and top up their wallets or live frugally till their next paycheck. For the vast majority of people, there were no paychecks and no social security.

An incident similar to the one that happened in the Shetland Islands also happened in Falmouth in Cornwall in 1762. Three ships that had returned from China brought with them all manner of goods that were unavailable or unaffordable in England. They moored and set up shop in the harbor, and people from miles around came to buy, or sometimes just to see, the Oriental silks, spirits, tea, porcelain, and other exotic items. The ships quickly sold out of everything, causing a cash shortage in Falmouth and the surrounding area.

The southern and eastern coasts of England even developed their own early versions of Rum Row. So lucrative was the illicit trade with England that Dutch gin distilleries and French brandy makers bought their own ships specifically for that purpose. Just like their rum-runner successors, they dropped anchor at a safe distance from shore and waited for small fishing boats and other vessels to come and see what they were selling. After learning the price, the smaller boats would either stock up or head back to shore and see how much business they could drum up.

It's an interesting diversion to consider how smuggled spirits were transported. One of the health hazards of buying imported illicit spirits was that they were bought and sold straight from the still. This would be 60 to 70 percent ABV (120–140 proof). Anyone who has sampled spirit of this strength when touring a distillery knows what that means. It does more than make your eyes water. A sip or two won't harm you, but drunk in large quantities, it will kill you. It must be diluted with pure water to a level that's safe and pleasurable to drink. However, transporting it undiluted takes up less space, so the smugglers or the buyers then have to dilute it afterward.

This is how brandy was invented. Wine from France was shipped to the Netherlands in concentrated form because it saved space, and it was reconstituted at the other end. The Dutch word for the liquor that arrived, awaiting dilution, was *brandewijn*. When it was found that this drink could be enjoyed in its own right, diluted less than wine, it became known as "brandywine" and eventually "brandy."

The effects of drinking undiluted spirits were shown in an incident that took place in 1811 at Harwich, still a major port on the east coast of England. A smuggling ship ran aground, giving the crew no choice but to throw some six hundred tubs overboard to lighten the load and refloat the ship. These particular tubs were found by soldiers at the nearby Landguard Fort. This was the site of the last opposed seaborne invasion of England, which the Dutch attempted in 1667. The soldiers commenced drinking the undiluted spirit, and four of them died.

So, what is a tub? Let the English author Thomas Hardy explain, as recorded in his diary:

While superintending the church music (from 1801 onward to about 1805) my grandfather used to do a little smuggling, his house being a lonely one, none of the others in Higher, or Upper, Bockhampton being then built. . . . He sometimes had as many as eighty tubs in a dark closet (afterwards destroyed in altering the staircase)—each containing four gallons. The spirits often smelt all over the house, being proof, and had to be lowered for drinking. The tubs, or little elongated barrels, were of thin staves with wooden hoops. (I remember one of them which had been turned into a bucket by knocking out one head and putting in a handle.) They were brought at night by men on horseback, "slung" or in carts. A whiplash across the window-pane would wake my grandfather at two or three in the morning, and he would dress and go down. Not a soul was there, but a heap of tubs loomed up in front of the door. He would set to work and stow them in the dark closet aforesaid, and nothing more would happen till dusk the following evening, when groups of dark, long-bearded fellows would arrive, and carry off the tubs in twos and fours slung over their shoulders.

So tubs were basically miniature barrels, each containing about four gallons and light enough that a man could carry two tied together and slung over his shoulder, front and back. Tied in this way, the tubs also could be easily carried on the back of a pony.

The other consideration when buying spirits straight from the still was that they were always clear, resembling vodka more than brandy, rum, or whiskey, which get their coloring from time spent in the barrel. Of course, the whiskey from illicit stills in Scotland was also clear, but many of the well-to-do customers expected their brandy to be the color of brandy, especially if would be served to guests, and even more especially if one of those guests was the local excise officer. The way around this was to add a drop of caramel or other coloring in each batch, which the distillery might do or a smuggler might add for certain customers before selling the spirit.

So how much illicit smuggling went on in Britain? In his enjoyable and well-researched book *Smuggling in the British Isles: A History* (and its companion website, www.smuggling.co.uk) author Richard Platt explains that the underground nature of smuggling makes it hard to be sure. But he lists a few examples of illicit transactions that were recorded, which indicate the huge scale of the operations:

- On one day in 1766 a single smuggler bought almost 110 imperial tons (123 US tons) of tea from a warehouse in Nantes, France.
- In one week in 1813, 12,000 gallons (54,500 liters) of brandy landed at Dungeness.

Platt also suggests the profits to be made: gin could be sold in the United Kingdom at four times the price it cost to buy in Europe, tobacco could be sold at about five times the cost, and tea for about ten times the purchase price. Although the figures would vary over time, that 110 tons of tea would have cost the smuggler almost £7,200, and he could have expected to sell it for at least £70,000. That's about £15 million ($19 million) in today's money. Even allowing for high expenses, he would have made a considerable profit.

There were also, of course, considerable risks. Being at sea, and even crossing the English Channel, was one of them. The channel has always been a busy shipping lane, a funnel that, even back then, was filled with ships that connected London with France, Spain, the United States, the Caribbean, Latin America, and Africa. These were joined by the smuggling trade, moving back and forth across the channel, crossing these shipping lanes. Smuggling ships were often painted black, used dark sails, and favored moonless nights in order to avoid detection. Because of this, they had to be especially vigilant while crossing the channel.

Once across, they had to make their way to the arranged rendezvous, often a deserted beach or a part of the coast with lots of bays and inlets to reduce the risk of detection. Coordinating meetings at such locations—being sure to be in the same place at the same time on a dark night, perhaps in heavy rain—could be confusing for the parties involved. Those on board watched for a signal from the shore to indicate that the coast was literally clear, an expression still in use today. A bonfire might be built on a beach to provide flames easily visible at sea, and unlucky customs officers who found the fire and put it out or otherwise attempted to interfere could be killed.

Other ingenious signaling methods were used to let boats know if it was safe to bring their cargo in. In the flat landscapes of the Norfolk Broads (ideal smuggling territory due to its confusing maze of waterways), local mill owners stopped their mills' sails at a particular angle to indicate safety and a different angle for danger. On Looe Island off the coast of Cornwall, a local farmer rode his distinctive white horse along the coast if all was clear, and then the islanders lit a blaze to beckon the ship. If customs officers were known to be around, people might light decoy fires a few miles from the drop-off location.

It was also difficult getting ships close to the shore or smaller boats onto the beach. Arrangements had to be in place so there were enough people to unload the often large amounts of contraband and then to spirit it away, so to speak, as quickly as possible to the intended destination. All this while watching for the authorities. If detected, the added drama and danger of gunfights or fistfights could occur.

Usually the smugglers had the advantage in numbers, with dozens if not hundreds of men compared to only a handful of customs officers. Those enormous profits meant that successful smugglers could afford to recruit large numbers of locals to transport goods or simply to provide intimidation. Here's one example recorded on September 18, 1873, about an incident at Cuckmere Haven in Sussex, on the south coast of England, which details the numbers that might be involved in such a venture:

> between two and three hundred smugglers on horseback came to Cookmere [*sic*] and received various kinds of goods from the boats, 'till at last the whole number were laden, when, in defiance of the King's officers, they went their way in great triumph. About a week before this, upwards of three hundred attended at the same place; and though the sea ran mountains high, the daring men in the cutters made good the landing.

Little wonder that the handfuls of excise men frequently did little more than look on, even if they knew about the operations in the first place. Another factor is that until the late seventeenth century, smuggling was a capital crime. Any smuggler faced with any customs officer had little to lose by attacking or even murdering the officer, as he faced death anyway if he was apprehended.

Another incident that indicates the numbers involved and the easy escalation into violence took place in 1784 near Christchurch in Dorset, on the south coast of England. It became known as the Battle of Mudeford. On July 15, two boats arrived, bringing contraband brandy and tea. An estimated three hundred people were busy unloading the cargo onto about fifty carts pulled by three hundred horses when the authorities arrived. This time, it was no mere handful of men, but a Royal Navy warship accompanied by two revenue cruisers.

The master of the warship HMS *Orestes*, William Allen, determined to either seize the cargo or destroy the smugglers' two boats, which by now were landed on the beach. Six rowing boats filled with heavily armed sailors were lowered, and they headed for the shore. Understandably, all was chaos among the smugglers, who were desperately trying to get the boats emptied of cargo and the cargo onto carts and away from the beach and the approaching sailors.

As the sailors neared the shore, Allen shouted to the smugglers, demanding their surrender. The smugglers answered with gunfire, mortally wounding Allen. They hadn't only been unloading the cargo; they had been digging trenches on the beach, which they hid behind and fired on the sailors in their open boats. The sailors kept coming, and as they reached the beach, the smugglers retreated to a nearby pub, Haven House (which is still there today). Here they holed up for several hours while the gun battle continued. The *Orestes* was also using its cannon to bombard the beach and the pub, though not with total accuracy, as some cannonballs hit Christchurch Priory, two miles (3.2 km) away.

Most of the smugglers escaped under cover of gunfire, and the cargo was never seized. It was estimated to be twenty-five tons of tea and 120,000 gallons of spirits. However, three of the smugglers were arrested and charged with the murder of William Allen. The charges were dropped against two of the men, but the third, George Coombes, was convicted and hanged. His body was hung in chains at Haven House Point as a deterrent to lawbreakers, but eventually it was taken down and given a proper burial.

The Christchurch Gang, as this bunch of smugglers was known, was a renowned and large smuggling ring, but typical of many others throughout the country. The gun battle and murder that took place at Mudeford was bigger and more serious than most, because of the arrival of the Royal Navy warship and two revenue boats. However, the chances of injury by gunshot, clubs, or fists were such that many of the larger rings made sure to include the local doctor among their number. Injuries could be treated with no questions asked and a case of whiskey by way of payment.

IS THERE AN INTERNATIONAL DEFINITION OF SMUGGLING?

There is an agreed international definition of smuggling. The United Nations Office on Drugs and Crime (UNODC) provides a comprehensive definition of smuggling of goods, including smuggling of drugs, firearms, counterfeit goods, alcohol, and other illegal commodities.

According to the UNODC, smuggling of goods refers to the illegal movement of goods across borders with the intention to evade customs duties, taxes, or other regulations. It involves the deliberate concealment, transportation, or possession of goods in violation of applicable laws or regulations.

Although the specific legal definitions and penalties for smuggling may vary from one country to another, the fundamental concept remains consistent across international borders, guided by various conventions, treaties, and agreements aimed at combating transnational organized crime and illicit trafficking.

Although this chapter focuses on the history of smuggling, it isn't a topic that's confined to the past. Smuggling is alive and well in all kinds of places. When the Soviet Union broke up in 1991, most of the distilleries were in Russia, leading to an illicit trade with breakaway countries like Estonia, Latvia, and Lithuania. This continued for many years, even after the breakaway countries had established their own vodka distilleries. Old habits die hard, especially criminal ones. Mostly they used the more direct means of underground pipelines rather than complicated clandestine operations.

In 2004, a two-mile pipeline was discovered that was transporting cheap vodka from Belarus to Lithuania, and in 2006 and 2008, pipelines were found to be sending cheap Russian vodka into Estonia. Then on the far side of the former Soviet Union in central Asia, another vodka pipeline was revealed in 2013. This one began in Kazakhstan, one of the main grain-producing nations in central Asia. And where there's grain, there's also cheap alcohol. This pipeline, a more modest 0.3 miles (0.5 km) long and eight inches (20 cm) wide, ran along the bottom of the River Chu, the border between Kazakhstan and Kyrgyzstan. The police in Kyrgyzstan who found the pipeline—the alcohol equivalent of an oil pipeline, with a series of valves controlling the flow—estimated that it had been used to send thousands of liters of illicit vodka into Kyrgyzstan.

More underground rivers of vodka were found after the Russian invasion of Ukraine in February 2022. A few months into the con-flict, the vigilant State Border Service of Ukraine discovered a short pipeline about 600 feet (183 m) long. They were on a routine patrol and noticed the distinctive smell of illicit hooch seeping from the polyethylene pipe. They filmed themselves filling a plastic bottle with the fast-flowing vodka, which was headed from the private home of a thirty-two-year-old Ukrainian citizen into neighboring Moldova. The video was uploaded to YouTube, where it started to go viral but was then removed, which seems a shame.

So, not even war, borders, legislation, or customs officers can stop the activities of determined smugglers, as we see in the next chapter, which looks specifically at the making of and trade in the infamous American moonshine. And we discover how the multimillion NASCAR organi-zation grew out of mom-and-pop moonshine makers.

· 3 ·

SHINE ON MOONSHINE

Moonshine (noun):
1. Informal. smuggled or illicitly distilled liquor, especially corn liquor as illicitly distilled chiefly in rural areas of the southern U.S.
2. empty or foolish talk, ideas, etc.; nonsense.
3. the light of the moon; moonlight.

Although moonshine has come to be associated mainly with illicit liquor made in the southern United States, the word can be used to describe any illicit spirit. So the liquor made in the secret stills of Scotland was moonshine as well as whiskey. Russian vodka sluiced down pipelines into other countries is also moonshine. Today's craft distilleries proudly describe some of their spirits as moonshine, though of course they're made legally; that's more marketing than factual.

In this chapter we concentrate on good old American moonshine, which can be made in any state in the nation. You don't necessarily need a license to distill your own spirits. In Arizona, for example, you are allowed to make your own spirits, provided you're giving them away only to family and friends aged twenty-one or older. You just can't sell them without a license (currently $1,850).

Making moonshine is not confined to hillbillies living off the grid in the rural South, either. You can make moonshine anywhere, including Alaska. In fact, you can buy the *Alaskan Bootlegger's Bible* on Amazon, if you're interested (more than four hundred five-star reviews!). The Alaskan climate does present problems for the distiller, as the initial fermentation process requires a certain temperature before the yeast will start its excellent work of turning sugars into alcohol. If you relied on natural heat, the Alaskan distilling season would be a very short one.

One bootlegger came up with a clever solution. He reckoned that putting a quarter stick of dynamite into the mix would kick-start the fermentation process. (Alaska is the kind of place where people have dynamite lying around in their sheds.) Unfortunately, ingesting any hint of nitroglycerin causes severe headaches, nausea, and fainting, so drinking dynamite moonshine wasn't exactly a blast.

Why do we call it "moonshine" in the first place? What's now seen as a very American term actually originated in England in the eighteenth century and was taken to the United States by British and Irish immigrants . . . along with their distilling skills. The word *moonshine* didn't last long in the British Isles, where people developed their own terms for illicit hooch. In Ireland, although the phrase Irish moonshine might be used, mostly they call it poitín. This derives from the Irish word *pota*, which means pot, referring to the little pot stills the distillers used.

In Scotland the word *peatreek* was commonly used, referring to the smoke, or reek, created by drying malted barley over a peat fire. Some commercial distillers now produce a moonshine-style whiskey and use peatreek or peat reek in the name. Reek is also used in a popular Scottish saying: "lang may yer lum reek." This means "long may your chimney smoke," and although it is a traditional wish to anyone buying a new house, it might equally apply to those illicit distillers that we came across in chapter 1.

One version of the derivation of the word *moonshine* claims that one time an illicit distiller was caught retrieving some of his whiskey from a local pond where he had hidden it. When caught in the act, he expressed surprise and pretended to be a simpleton, pointing at the moon's reflection and claiming that he was looking for the big cheese that was at the bottom of the pond. That does seem rather far-fetched and fanciful, and it's far more likely that the word was used to describe any kind of illicit activity carried out under the cover of darkness, with only the light of the moon to show what was going on. As the making and smuggling of illicit liquor was just about the biggest illegal activity requiring secrecy, moonshine and moonshiners became associated with the business of unlawful booze.

POITÍN

Poitín (pronounced poe-teen) is a traditional Irish distilled spirit, often referred to as Irish moonshine or Irish whiskey's illicit cousin. It's one of the oldest distilled drinks in Europe, with roots dating back to the sixth century. Poitín is made from malted barley, grain, potatoes, sugar beet, treacle, and other ingredients.

Historically, poitín was produced illegally in small home stills across rural Ireland, primarily in remote areas where authorities had difficulty enforcing the law. The distillation of poitín was outlawed in the seventeenth century by the English Crown as a means of taxation and control. Despite this prohibition, poitín continued to be produced clandestinely for centuries, with its production and consumption deeply ingrained in Irish rural culture.

The name poitín is derived from the Irish word *pota*, which means pot. Traditionally, poitín was made in small pot stills, giving it a distinctive flavor and potency. It's typically much stronger than commercial spirits, often ranging from 40 percent to 90 percent alcohol by volume (ABV), though it can be diluted to lower strengths.

In recent years, there's been a resurgence of interest in traditional Irish spirits and artisanal distillation methods. Poitín has benefited from this renewed interest, with some producers now legally producing and marketing it.

Of course, there are many other words used to describe the homemade stuff, including white lightning, firewater, and mountain dew, and some more imaginative descriptions such as rattlesnake milk, stump juice, swamp gravy, popskull, red-eye, liquid thunder, and forty-rod (because moonshine could kill you from a distance of forty rods [220 yards]). Some of the characters involved in the moonshine business have equally vivid names and stories to match. One of the best-known of these was Marvin "Popcorn" Sutton.

Sutton got his nickname only indirectly due to his love of popcorn. He was trying to get some out of a machine while playing a game of pool, but the popcorn machine wasn't working so he attacked it with his cue. He was born in 1946 in Maggie Valley, a small town in North Carolina's prime moonshine country. Like those illicit Scottish distillers who believed it was their right to make whiskey from their own grain without paying tax on it, Sutton believed that making moonshine was part of his heritage, and nobody's business but his.

That isn't surprising, since Sutton was himself of mixed Irish and Scottish descent, and both his father and his grandfather were bootleggers who taught him how to make moonshine at an early age. Making moonshine was just as much a part of his North Carolina heritage, too: it has been called the second-oldest profession in the state. It's been made there for at least three centuries, ever since the first European immigrants arrived with their wicked ways and showed the local people that there was more you could do with corn than just eat it. The Tar Heel state hasn't been the same since.

Like those illicit distillers in Scotland and Ireland, Sutton continually bobbed and weaved to stay one step ahead of the authorities. He didn't always succeed. In 1974, he was convicted of selling untaxed liquor and put on probation. In 1981, he was charged with felony possession of a controlled substance and was put on probation with a five-year suspended sentence. Then in 1985, he was convicted of felony assault with a deadly weapon (and not with a cue this time) and was sentenced to three years at Craggy Correctional Center in Asheville.

Sutton then enjoyed a good run without falling afoul of the law again till 1998. That was when his legitimate business, a roadside junk shop, was searched and found to contain a still and sixty gallons of moonshine. This time, he got probation and another suspended sentence. The following year, he produced and self-published both a book and a video that were part autobiography and part guide to making moonshine titled *Me and My Likker*.

Fame was also on its way. In 2002, he appeared in a documentary film made by Neal Hutcheson called *Mountain Talk*, which dealt with the local mountain dialect known as Appalachian English. Having met Sutton, Hutcheson wasted no time in making another film that same year, exclusively about Popcorn, titled with a phrase that Sutton used more than once in his life: *This is the Last Dam Run of Likker I'll Ever Make.* You can find it on YouTube if you're interested.

APPALACHIAN ENGLISH

Appalachian English, also known as Appalachian dialect or Appalachian English dialect, refers to the variety of English spoken in the Appalachian region of the United States. This region spans parts of around thirteen states, including portions of Alabama, Georgia, Kentucky, Maryland, Mississippi, New York, North Carolina, Ohio, Pennsylvania, South Carolina, Tennessee, Virginia, and West Virginia.

Appalachian English is characterized by several distinctive features, many of which stem from the historical settlement patterns of the region, as well as the influence of Irish, Scottish, English, and German immigrants who settled there during the eighteenth and nineteenth centuries.

Some key features of Appalachian English include:

1. Vocabulary: Appalachian English includes unique vocabulary that may not be commonly used in other varieties of English. Some words and phrases are borrowed from Scotch-Irish, Scottish Gaelic, and other languages spoken by early settlers.

2. Pronunciation: Appalachian English may exhibit distinct pronunciation patterns, such as the pronunciation of certain vowels and consonants, as well as unique intonation patterns.

3. Grammar: Appalachian English may have distinct grammatical features, including unique word order, verb forms, and sentence structures.

4. Syntax: Appalachian English may exhibit unique syntactic features, including the use of double modals (e.g., "might could"), the absence of the verb "to be" in certain constructions (e.g., "He sick"), and other syntactic patterns influenced by Scotch-Irish and other immigrant languages.

5. Expressions and idioms: Like any regional dialect, Appalachian English includes a variety of expressions, idioms, and sayings that are specific to the region.

It's important to note that Appalachian English is not one single dialect but rather a diverse and dynamic variety of English that can vary significantly from one community to another within the Appalachian region. Additionally, due to various social, economic, and cultural factors, the use of Appalachian English may change over time, with some features becoming more or less prominent.

For the likker maker, 2007 was another busy year. The good news was that he featured in a History Channel documentary called *Hillbilly: The Real Story*, but the bad news was that there was a fire at a property he owned in Parrotsville, Tennessee. The firefighters put out the fire, but while doing so, they discovered 650 gallons of Sutton's likker. Popcorn was on probation again.

In 2008, the story sours. He was still on probation when an undercover agent for the Tennessee Alcoholic Beverage Commission (TABC) got Sutton to reveal that he had 500 gallons of moonshine in Tennessee and another 400 gallons in Maggie Valley, all for sale. Sutton pleaded guilty to distilling spirits illegally, to felony possession of a firearm, to tax evasion, and to transportation of an illegal substance.

He was handed eighteen months in federal prison, which he asked to serve under house arrest on the grounds that he was now sixty-two and had a serious medical condition. He had reportedly had a mental breakdown upon being told that he had cancer. The judge refused, saying that Sutton was already on probation when he committed the latest offenses and had been on probation so many times in the past without effect that a jail sentence was the only option. He said he had already provided some clemency by sentencing Sutton to only eighteen months when he should have been given two years.

It was too much for Sutton, who this time really had made his "last dam run of likker." On March 16, 2009, a few days before he was due to surrender himself to the authorities to start his jail sentence, he committed suicide by carbon monoxide poisoning in his car. He had served time once and didn't intend to do it again, preferring to die as he had lived, by defying the authorities and making his own decisions. In 2014, Neal Hutcheson made another documentary about this larger-than-life character, with the appropriate title of *Popcorn Sutton— A Hell of a Life*.

Sutton's legacy lives on, though, in the shape of—or rather the taste of—Popcorn Sutton's Tennessee White Whiskey. After Sutton's death, his widow Pam and country star Hank Williams Jr. (who attended Sutton's memorial service) signed an agreement to produce a whiskey using Sutton-designed stills and his own secret recipe. But controversy followed Sutton beyond the grave. In 2013, the makers were sued by Jack Daniel's, which claimed that the bottle's shape and label too closely resembled its own. In 2014, the lawsuit was settled out of court for an undisclosed sum, and the bottles and labels were substantially redesigned.

In 2014, Popcorn Sutton Distilling acquired its own distillery and during the next couple of years recruited a couple of distillers from the prestigious George Dickel Distillery, though soon afterward the physical distillery (but not the brand names) was sold to the huge Sazerac alcoholic beverage company. In 2023, Popcorn's whiskey rose again from the ashes as Popcorn Sutton Original Small Batch Recipe, distilled just a few miles from his final home in Tennessee. I wonder what the cantankerous old moonshiner with a colorful vocabulary would have to say about his name being used to make "likker" legally? It probably couldn't be repeated here.

SOME APPALACHIAN ENGLISH EXPRESSIONS

1. "Fixin' to": Meaning "about to" or "getting ready to." Example: "I'm fixin' to head down to the store."

2. "Bless your heart": A phrase used to express sympathy or pity, often used sarcastically. Example: "She's been sick for weeks, bless her heart."

3. "Over yonder": Referring to a location that is nearby but not precisely specified. Example: "The creek's just over yonder by the old oak tree."

4. "Gettin' on": Referring to aging or getting older. Example: "He's really gettin' on in years now."

5. "Tump over": Meaning to tip or overturn something. Example: "Be careful not to tump over that bucket."

6. "Holler": A small valley between mountains or hills. Example: "They live up the holler, past the old mill."

7. "Ain't got a pot to piss in": Referring to someone who is extremely poor or lacking resources. Example: "They're so broke, they ain't got a pot to piss in."

8. "Slick as a whistle": Meaning very smooth or slippery. Example: "The road was slick as a whistle after the rain."

9. "Cattywampus": Meaning askew or not straight. Example: "That picture's hangin' all cattywampus on the wall."

10. "Gumption": Referring to initiative, resourcefulness, or common sense. Example: "You've got to have some gumption to survive out here."

Popcorn Sutton may have led a hell of a life, but he's far from being the only moonshiner who did. Another was Alvin Sawyer, who became known as the moonshine king of the Great Dismal Swamp. For those who don't know it, the Great Dismal Swamp isn't a location from *Lord of the Rings* but a national wildlife refuge that covers more than one hundred thousand acres of Virginia and North Carolina. It's the perfect place for moonshiners to operate—at least those who are undeterred by the black bears, twenty-two types of snakes, and other critters that also make the place their home. There are also alligators nearby that are said to be edging closer to the swamp each year.

THE GREAT DISMAL SWAMP

The Great Dismal Swamp is a large marshy area located in the southeastern United States, primarily in southeastern Virginia and northeastern North Carolina. It spans approximately 190 square miles (490 square kilometers) and is known for its dense vegetation, diverse wildlife, and historical significance.

1. Geography: The Great Dismal Swamp is characterized by its vast wetlands, including swamps, marshes, and forests. It's situated in a low-lying coastal plain and crisscrossed by numerous streams and rivers, including the Dismal Swamp Canal.

2. Flora and Fauna: The swamp is home to a wide variety of plant and animal species. It provides habitat for numerous bird species, such as the prothonotary warbler and the bald eagle, as well as mammals like black bears and bobcats. The vegetation includes dense stands of Atlantic white cedar, cypress, tupelo gum, and various types of ferns and mosses.

3. History: The Great Dismal Swamp has a rich history dating back thousands of years. Native American tribes, including the Nansemond and Chowanoke, inhabited the region and utilized its resources for hunting, fishing, and gathering. During the seventeenth and eighteenth centuries, European settlers began to exploit the swamp for its timber, which was highly valued for shipbuilding.

4. Escape Route: The swamp also played a significant role in African American history, serving as a refuge for escaped slaves seeking freedom. Fugitive slaves, known as maroons, established hidden communities within the swamp, living off the land and evading capture. These communities existed for generations, with some estimates suggesting that thousands of people lived in the Great Dismal Swamp during the antebellum period. This was the period from the late eighteenth century until the outbreak of the Civil War in 1861.

5. Dismal Swamp Canal: In the early nineteenth century, efforts were made to drain and develop the swamp for agricultural purposes. The Dismal Swamp Canal, completed in 1805, was constructed to facilitate transportation and commerce through the region. Today, the canal is part of the Atlantic Intracoastal Waterway and is still used for shipping and recreational boating.

6. Conservation: In the twentieth century, growing recognition of the ecological importance of the Great Dismal Swamp led to conservation efforts to protect its natural resources. In 1973, the Great Dismal Swamp National Wildlife Refuge was established to preserve and manage the swamp's diverse ecosystems.

Alvin Sawyer operated stills in several remote areas of the swamp, with the presence of those poisonous snakes undoubtedly helping to reduce the chances of raids. Sawyer had other nicknames, but all confirming his status as the moonshine king of somewhere or other. At different times he was called the moonshine king of eastern North Carolina and the moonshine king of the Albemarle, the region of North Carolina from which Sawyer hailed. The Albemarle Sound was also perfect for bootlegging, with several rivers providing pure freshwater for distilling, and the maze of rivers, streams, and creeks offering getaway routes as well as a water network to deliver batches of moonshine to a number of small ports for distribution.

THE ALBEMARLE SOUND

The Albemarle Sound is a large estuarine body of water in North Carolina. It is one of the prominent features of the Albemarle-Pamlico Sound System, which is the second-largest estuarine system in the United States, after the Chesapeake Bay. The Albemarle Sound covers an area of approximately 640 square miles (1,658 square kilometers) and is fed by several rivers, including the Chowan, Roanoke, and Pasquotank Rivers.

The sound is characterized by its shallow depths and marshy shorelines, making it an important habitat for various species of fish, shellfish, and wildlife. It serves as a nursery ground for many commercially important species and supports a rich ecosystem.

Sawyer began making moonshine in 1934 at the age of fifteen while working at a sawmill. He later worked as a master welder in the Norfolk Shipyard (a handy skill for a moonshiner) and served in the Marine Corps during World War II, when his distilling skills were doubtlessly also put to use.

In all, Sawyer spent more than fifty years making moonshine, and even after he had retired, he began selling miniature nonworking stills whose brochures included a history of moonshine and a moonshine recipe. However, a year after he claimed to have retired, a full-sized, functional still was found on his property, resulting in a newspaper headline: "Moonshine king on the lam again." Arrest warrants were out for Sawyer and his son Johnny, and not for the first time. Alvin had served prison terms in both 1950 and 1951 but then had a clear run till 1985, when he was found in possession of three 500-gallon stills. Such equipment is capable of producing six barrels of moonshine a day if fully operational. This time, Sawyer was only put on probation for three years.

Nothing deterred him, though, and two years into his probationary period, he was arrested for possessing a 2,000-gallon still (eight barrels a day) and handed a four-month sentence. It was the biggest still ever found in the Great Dismal Swamp.

Sawyer certainly never gave himself up easily. On one occasion, Alcoholic Beverage Control (ABC) officers found one of his moonshine operations under the floor of his house and were looking forward to an arrest when Sawyer jumped out of the window and disappeared for a while. He also kept a still in one of his outhouses and disguised the smell of liquor by keeping hogs around it.

On another occasion when one of his stills was found in the Great Dismal Swamp, the officers took Sawyer onto their boat. However, they got lost in the maze of waterways, so Sawyer offered to drive the boat and get them out. When he took the wheel, he rammed the boat into a bank instead and skedaddled. On another similar occasion, he simply jumped off the boat. Failing to find any sign of him, the officers assumed he had drowned and moved on. When the coast was clear, Sawyer emerged from under the hollow log where he'd been hiding, breathing via an air pocket in the log.

On the occasions when they did manage to arrest Sawyer without him going on the lam, several of the arrests were made by the same officer, Benny Halstead of the Pasquotank ABC, who is said to have arrested more than twelve hundred bootleggers during his career. Ironically, toward the ends of their lives, both men ended up living in the same nursing home. They greatly respected one another as people, despite the fact that Halstead had sent Sawyer to prison no less than three times. Halstead said he thought Sawyer was a good man without an enemy in the world apart from the law. The other side of Sawyer was the devout Christian who taught Sunday School and delivered the occasional sermon from the pulpit of his local church. Nor did he drink. He made moonshine to make money, not to drink it. This was also true of bootlegger George Remus, who we meet in chapter 4 and who was known (inevitably) as the bourbon king.

There were certainly enough people who did drink to keep the moonshiners busy and happy, though, and many had more cash stashed away than their hillbilly appearance would suggest. And as we've seen in the first two chapters, the story of moonshine is inextricably linked with tax laws and wars. Just as in England and Scotland, the first taxes ever levied on alcohol in the United States were to finance a war. This time, it was the Civil War, which began in April 1861. Fifteen months later, Congress passed an act that resulted in the creation of the Office of Internal Revenue, and in 1863 the first tax on distilled spirits was introduced. This was 20 cents a gallon, equivalent to about $5 today.

That might not seem a huge amount, but it was the thin end of the wedge. Two years later in 1865, that 20 cents became $1.50 (more than $35 today), and the following year it increased to $2 ($50), and in 1868 to $4 ($100 today). A gallon of whiskey fills roughly five 75-centiliter bottles, so that's today's equivalent of $20 tax on every bottle. Today in the United States, the tax payable on a 75-centiliter bottle of whiskey is $2.14. No wonder these taxes were a boon to the US moonshine industry, just as they had been in Scotland and England.

Business boomed, and would continue to boom for almost 100 years, across the so-called Moonshine Belt of Alabama, Georgia, Mississippi, North Carolina, South Carolina, Tennessee, and Virginia.

At the time, the government certainly needed the money. By the end of the war, government debt had reached $2.6 billion, which was forty times greater than it had been five years earlier. The moonshiners weren't about to chip in any time soon, though. They had dollar signs in their eyes as production grew and then grew again during the years of Prohibition. Prohibition began only fifty-five years after the end of the Civil War, though they seem to be from very different eras.

Moonshining rolled right on after Prohibition, too. One North Carolina newspaper, the *Murfreesboro Daily News*, reported on September 2, 1951: "The four Coastal plains counties of Hertford, Bertie, Northampton and Gates do more than a million dollars a year in bootleg whiskey business and between 1000 to 1500 unlicensed distilleries keep a steady flow of white lightning going to local and out-of-the-area thirsty moonshine guzzler[s]." Those figures were based on interviews with local law enforcement officers and related to just four counties in North Carolina. North Carolina has one hundred counties in all, and there were seven states in the Moonshine Belt. Not all produced at that level, but it was certainly big business, whichever way you do the math.

In one of those four counties mentioned, Bertie, some twenty years later in May 1972, one of the biggest stills ever found in North Carolina was uncovered in the small and innocently named rural community of Merry Hill. What appeared to be a residential mobile home, complete with playground equipment and a family dog, actually disguised a moonshine factory capable of producing 500 gallons of moonshine a day, or around 2,500 regular-sized bottles.

Manufacture began in November 1970, and in the eighteen months of its existence, it had produced more than 150,000 gallons of moonshine and deprived the authorities of precisely $1,612,353.70 in tax revenue. A consortium of several people, each of whom had their own specific responsibilities, ran the factory, just as with any legal organization. Two members of the group, a married couple, bought the mobile home for $10,544.40 and signed a five-year lease on a lot for $20 a month. The landlord had no idea that they were anything but an ordinary married couple. The essential services were installed, and the couple moved in, using false names.

The factory was then slowly constructed below and behind the home, though no one knows how the group managed to move the equipment in without being spotted and raising suspicion. The ingredients needed were also substantial, and somehow they had to bring thousands of empty jugs in and take thousands of full ones out. The fact that they got away with such a large-scale operation for eighteen months is a testimony to their careful planning, and if the tax revenue they got away with was more than $1.6 million, just imagine how much they made. When the case eventually went to trial, some of the gang and their suppliers were found not guilty, and others were sentenced to up to five years in prison. However, on appeal, the prison sentences were reduced to probation. The money had long disappeared. Sometimes it seems that crime does pay.

An even bigger factory was found near the small town of Midland in North Carolina in March 1968. It was cleverly concealed underneath a hay barn, the only access being a trapdoor that was naturally covered with hay. The disguise was so good that an earlier raid had failed to find it. The underground bunker measured 12 feet by 118 feet (3.7m × 36m) and contained twelve huge tanks, thousands of quart jars, hundreds of pounds of sugar and yeast, more than 700 gallons of moonshine, and more than 7,000 gallons of mash ready to be distilled into moonshine. The factory was capable of producing an estimated 600 gallons of moonshine *every day*.

Not all moonshiners are factory sized, though, and not all are following in the family business, as the case of two junior high school students demonstrated. This also happened in those North Carolina coastal plains counties in June 1960, and they can blame the movies for their short moonshine career. The boys and their dates went to a drive-in movie and parked in the back row. One of the boys recognized the whiff of moonshine wafting from a creek just behind them, whose only access was through the drive-in.

The two boys returned the next night in a van belonging to one of their fathers. They parked in the back row again (probably earning a few strange looks in the conservative South) and, during the movie, slipped out to follow the path to the creek, which was clearly being regularly used. Making sure no one was around, they found the still and put it in the back of their van. They then made their own moonshine for the next two years and sold their liquor to a local bootlegger known as Red Horse, who sold it to bars in Baltimore and Washington, DC.

They made enough money to pay their way through college, and if they didn't win an award for being the most enterprising students of the year, they should have. One eventually graduated with a law degree from the University of North Carolina at Chapel Hill, and the other graduated from Virginia Tech with a degree in civil engineering. With those qualifications, they clearly could have gone on to build bigger stills—and been assured of a good legal defense if charged—but instead they put their moonshining days behind them.

High school kids in North Carolina are clearly made of different stuff. Summer jobs picking fruit or vegetables or stocking shelves in a Piggly-Wiggly aren't for them. No, in North Carolina, some get jobs hauling moonshine or even helping to make it, although they must need to be both creative and careful when it comes to writing their resumes and applying for jobs.

In major moonshine areas, people made their money in different ways, like the auto mechanic known as Jelly Belly, who spent thirty-five years providing bootleggers with souped-up cars designed to both conceal heavy loads of liquor and yet still leave the police eating dirt at the side of the road. False rear seats were installed in some cars; in others, the fuel tanks held liquor and a replacement fuel tank was concealed beneath the car. The theory was that no cop or agent would look into a fuel tank expecting to find moonshine. If a driver did see a roadblock ahead, they might well abandon the car and make an escape. It was reckoned that moonshiners could afford to lose one car in three and still make a good profit.

Jelly Belly operated his garage in an isolated part of Northampton County in North Carolina, close to the state line shared with Virginia. Bootleggers' drivers took an interest in the whereabouts of state lines. When it came to cars, though, it's reported that they preferred 1949 Fords with Rocket 88 or Cadillac engines; later, they chose 1955 Chevrolets.

Naturally, driving the vehicles and making the most of these modified hotrods required great talents, and one of the greatest moonshine drivers of them all was Junior Johnson. These moonshine drivers had to really hone their skills, since they frequently drove during the darkest nights (moonshiners didn't really like the shine of the moon), on the backest of back roads while watching for bends and cops. They also had to get the best of a chase, lest they lose their load and then their job. It's no surprise then that the drivers who learned these skills in the 1930s and 1940s were in great demand when NASCAR came along in 1948.

Junior Johnson was born in 1931 in Ronda, a speck of a town in North Carolina. His family, of Ulster Scots descent, settled in North Carolina in the eighteenth century and quickly got into the whiskey business. Johnson's father died at the age of sixty-three, having spent twenty of those years in prison for bootlegging, but it didn't deter Junior (full name: Robert Glenn Johnson Jr.) from following in his footsteps—and his tire tracks—by becoming a driver for moonshiners in the 1940s. He didn't even have a driver's license when he started. He didn't know it, of course, but he was in training to become a NASCAR legend.

Junior never got caught while transporting moonshine; he was just too good a driver. The one time he did get arrested, it was for having a still. He spent a year in prison from 1956 to 1957, by which time he was already a successful NASCAR driver. He started driving NASCAR in 1955, won five races, and finished sixth in the overall rankings. From 1956 to 1957, he was otherwise occupied, but in 1958 he won six NASCAR races.

In 1960, he competed in the Daytona 500 and won his first long-distance race. He did this by inventing the technique of slipstreaming, or drafting. He knew his car was a few miles per hour slower than the top cars in the race, and when one of those cars passed him during a test run, Johnson happened to move in behind it. He noticed that his car's speed picked up due to the slipstream effect. He stayed in the car's slipstream until almost the end of the test run, when he used a kind of slingshot technique to catapult himself past the faster car. Johnson not only won the test run, but he won the main race, too, despite having a slower car. That's what you call driving.

Johnson went on to become a NASCAR owner and an entrepreneur. In 1973, Jeff Bridges portrayed him in a fictionalized version of his life,

NASCAR TODAY IN FACTS AND FIGURES

1. As of 2021, NASCAR (National Association for Stock Car Auto Racing) is reportedly worth more than $3.2 billion.
2. NASCAR's media rights are valued at more than $8.2 billion, collected from a ten-year deal signed with NBC Sports and Fox Sports in 2013.
3. Nearly 358 million people watched NASCAR live in 2020, with an average of 860,000 viewers per race.
4. Higher level sponsorships in the Cup Series cost between $5 million and $35 million.
5. The 2020 Daytona 500 drew more than seven million viewers.
6. The top NASCAR drivers are worth millions. For example, as of 2021, Jimmie Johnson had an estimated net worth of $160 million, and Dale Earnhardt Jr.'s net worth is estimated at about $300 million.

and in 1986 President Ronald Reagan pardoned his moonshining conviction. In 2007, he returned to making moonshine—legally, this time. He partnered with Piedmont Distillers of North Carolina, the only legal distillery in the state at that time and the first since Prohibition, to create Midnight Moon, a moonshine made in the traditional Johnson family way. Johnson passed away in 2019 at the age of eighty-eight while in hospice care and suffering from Alzheimer's. It was a sad end to a long and adventurous life, and you can drink a toast to him with Midnight Moon, which you can still buy at www.piedmontdistillers.com.

Despite the incredible stories about people like Junior Johnson, Popcorn Sutton, and Alvin Sawyer, perhaps the greatest moonshiner of them all was Joshua Percy Flowers. Dubbed the king of the moonshiners by *The Saturday Evening Post*, Flowers was estimated to have earned an annual $1 million in untaxed income during the height of his moonshining years.

Flowers was born in 1903 in Wilson, North Carolina. He quickly showed an astute business sense and began buying plots of land during the Great Depression with the intention of growing cotton and tobacco. This he did until the 1970s, which helped to explain the lavish donations that he gave to his local church, the White Oak Baptist Church. Not all the money for this and other generous philanthropic gifts came from cotton and tobacco, though. On one of his properties, a five-thousand-acre farm, he also grew corn and set up a moonshine factory.

The Flowers moonshine operation was huge. Trucks from the big northern cities like Washington, Philadelphia, and Baltimore, picked up thousands of bottles at a time. His church can hardly have been unaware of how Flowers made his money, since he was indicted ten times by federal grand juries and eighteen times at the state and local levels, though he seems to have spent precious little time in prison. Perhaps his friendships with local politicians and those generous donations to various worthy causes helped.

An example of the Flowers "luck" was in 1935, when he had his first run-in with the law. It wasn't directly related to distilling, but because he and his brothers had an encounter with a federal treasury agent, whom they beat up. They were all sent to prison, but Flowers was released after three days. His lawyer had appealed to the judge on the grounds that Percy Flowers was a large landowner with no fewer than twenty-two sharecropping families depending on him to make a living. For whatever reason, the judge listened to him and set Flowers free.

It wasn't till 1957 that Flowers received the longest jail sentence he would serve: six months. A store that Flowers operated was raided, resulting in the seizure of his safe, which contained large amounts of cash. The jury was divided on the main charges brought against Flowers. Unfortunately, Flowers couldn't control his temper and engaged in a verbal set-to with a treasury agent in the courthouse lobby, whereupon the judge found him guilty of contempt of court.

The colorful life of Percy Flowers is recounted in the book *Lost Flowers* by his son, Perry D. Sullivan. Published in 2013, it is unfortunately now out of print, though at the time of this writing, you could pick up a secondhand copy on Amazon for a mere $79.

A book that is more readily available and highly recommended is *North Carolina Moonshine: An Illicit History* by Frank Stephenson Jr. and Barbara Nichols Mulder. Stephenson's father was a Hertford County deputy in North Carolina, and his son went on many a moonshine raid with him while growing up. He describes approaching a suspected bootlegging operation in which they could smell the moonshine and hear the hissing of a still. They approached the yard quietly to find that the still was doing its business while, alongside it, a naked man and woman were also doing their business. Stephenson Sr. fired his gun, the human business came to a premature end, and the woman grabbed two empty sugar bags and hid behind a barrel to try to preserve what was left of her modesty.

Perhaps just as surprising was another raid on a still that was operating behind a church. Father and son again found the likely location and followed their noses to track down the still and the moonshine. To their surprise, they found the minister of the church, along with his wife and their two young daughters, operating the still. While he was working, the minister hummed "What a Friend We Have in Jesus." Well, if Jesus could turn water into wine, why not turn corn into moonshine? The dilapidated state of the church illustrated their need for the money.

Making moonshine made for many strange contradictions like this. Frank Stephenson Jr. recounts a conversation he had with one bootlegger: "I shore did make it and a lot of it, and I am proud as hell that I did. I sent all three of my children to college on the money that I made off moonshine."

Such incongruities were nothing compared to the outright hypocrisy of the Prohibition era, as we see in the next chapter. Prohibition was the period when laws aimed at reducing people's drinking habits only made alcohol all the more desirable, and the lawmakers at the heart of those laws were among the worst lawbreakers. You didn't think the White House stayed dry during Prohibition, did you?

· 4 ·

PROHIBITION

The word *prohibition* automatically suggests the years from 1920 to 1933, when Prohibition existed in the United States. But over the years, prohibition of alcohol (though it can apply to anything banned) has been introduced in many countries around the world. Indeed, in countries like Afghanistan, Saudi Arabia, and Yemen, prohibition is a permanent way of life.

In other countries, prohibition has come and gone, or only applies to certain people and groups or during certain times. In Malaysia, prohibition applies only to Muslims, but alcohol is available everywhere. In Thailand, the sale of alcohol is banned during elections, on certain days of the year, and at certain times of day, although hotels and resorts are exempt from the rules. In Venezuela, the sale (but not the consumption) of alcohol is also banned prior to elections and during Holy Week. And those intrepid drinkers, the Brits, have never felt the need for prohibition.

In Russia under the czars, prohibition movements were in fact political antigovernment movements, as Mark Lawrence Schrad explains in his hefty and thorough book, *Smashing the Liquor Machine: A Global History of Prohibition*. The czars had a monopoly on alcohol. If a Russian serf wanted a shot of vodka, he could only get it from a state-sanctioned bar. Moonshining was quashed by the authorities. Serfs would get themselves in debt by drinking to excess, and the only way they could pay it off was by signing over next year's crops.

The money raised by the sale of vodka across that vast land provided the funds for the czar's lavish lifestyle and most of the costs of running their courts and the country. Reformers saw that the only way they could improve the lot of the people was by stopping drinking. Not only would it solve a social problem, since many people drank themselves to oblivion, but it would put a dent in the czars' main source of income. Temperance advocates were therefore antigovernment protestors, and troops would be sent in to deal with them.

Alcohol wasn't initially such a contentious issue in the United States, but there were some parallels with the Russian situation in the years leading to Prohibition, notably the social problems caused by excessive alcohol consumption. When the Pilgrims arrived on the *Mayflower* in 1620, they brought with them beer and hard liquor and the knowledge and means to make them. Alcohol was simply a part of their diet. Beer and cider were preferred over water because they were more sanitary at a time when water supplies could not be guaranteed to be pure. It was far safer to ferment or distill grain to produce a purified beverage than to risk sickness or even death by drinking contaminated water.

It's known that the Pilgrims landed in Massachusetts because they were running out of beer, but that fact is easily misinterpreted. They had brought water with them, but the water supply became contaminated, leaving only beer. Drinking beer is dehydrating, although it's better than not drinking at all. When the beer began to run out, the Pilgrims knew that they would have to land and replenish their supplies of both beer and water. They landed and liked what they saw and founded New Plymouth, having sailed from Plymouth in England. They had only water to drink, though, until they started brewing their own beer. The first Thanksgiving was therefore almost certainly alcohol free.

Puritans were not puritanical about alcohol. Distilling and brewing was as much a part of their lives as growing crops and keeping chickens. Drinks like beer, spirits, and wine were all seen as God given, although drinking to excess was very much frowned upon. And it was drinking to excess, many years later, that helped make Prohibition happen.

The other contentious subject in this balancing act is taxation. In fact, taxation caused a rebellion in only the second year of George Washington's first term of office, when a tax on distilled spirits was introduced. It applied to all spirits, but at that time whiskey was becoming the dominant spirit, so it became widely known as the whiskey tax. The ensuing revolt became known as the Whiskey Rebellion or the Whiskey Insurrection.

The whiskey tax, which began in 1791, was the first tax on a domestic product to be introduced by the newly created federal government. The tax was proposed by the secretary of the treasury, Alexander Hamilton, to help pay off the war debt that had accrued during the American War of Independence. The UK government adopted a similar tactic seven years later when the country's first-ever income tax was enacted to pay for weapons and preparations for the impending Napoleonic Wars.

In the United States, it was initially farmers who objected to the tax. They had long been distilling their excess grain crops like barley, rye, or corn to make whiskey. Whiskey was also commonly used as a form of barter, a trade unpopular with governments, since no cash changes hands, making it hard to levy taxes on the transaction. Many of the farmers were also veterans of the War of Independence who, having fought for freedom, protested paying tax on something they had previously freely produced.

Although the protests began in 1791, it wasn't until 1794 that matters reached a head, and a conclusion, in Western Pennsylvania. Here farmers and distillers resorted to using violence to prevent federal officials from collecting the hated tax. The government sent a US marshal to serve writs to those who had not paid the tax. A gang of five hundred armed men, having heard news of the marshal's impending arrival, attacked the home of John Neville, the federal tax inspector whose responsibility it was to collect the tax.

The government's response was swift and blunt. First, negotiators were sent to try to reason with the protestors, but the president simultaneously raised an army of thirteen thousand men who had no intention of reasoning. Washington himself led the troops, but the protestors dispersed before the army arrived. Seeing the strength of the government's response, some farmers and distillers reluctantly began to pay the whiskey tax, and those who didn't were taken to court.

The tax, unpopular and difficult to collect, was eventually repealed in 1802. The memory lingers on, though. In 2011 the city of Washington, Pennsylvania, introduced the Whiskey Rebellion Festival, which included historic reenactments, such as the tarring and feathering of a tax inspector.

A significant date in the movement toward Prohibition was the creation of the Prohibition Party in 1869, only fifteen years after the founding of the Republican Party, making it the third-oldest political party in the United States. Yes, the party still exists, and it received 4,834 votes in the 2020 presidential election out of 158 million votes cast, or 0.003 percent. Sadly, its members can't have a consolation drink afterward.

The party did better in its early days, though, its best year being 1872, when it picked up 270,879 votes, or 2.24 percent of the total votes cast. In 1874 another campaigning group was founded, the Women's Christian Temperance Union (WCTU), followed in 1893 by the Anti-Saloon League. The American Temperance Society had already been established back in 1826.

Undoubtedly, excessive drinking had become a problem by the nineteenth century. America had moved a long way from the moderate drinking of the Pilgrims. It wasn't called the Wild West for nothing. As the frontier moved ever westward, towns like Tombstone and Dodge City became notorious for their riotous saloons, bordellos, and liquor-fueled poker games.

Then, as the country became more industrialized, drinking became the new norm for some working men. It wasn't that everyone drank, but those who did made up for those who didn't. Families suffered when too many wage earners spent their money on liquor rather than food. Wives were abused or abandoned, husbands were ending up on the streets, and children were suffering for lack of a proper family upbringing.

During the years between 1800 and 1830, American drinking was at its peak. It was still the case that water could be contaminated, healthier drinks like fresh milk were hard to come by, and others like tea and coffee were more expensive than whiskey. It wasn't unusual for families to start the day with a little beer or cider—or even whiskey—with their breakfast. Workers were given breaks when they could enjoy a quick drink, and babies were given a little light alcoholic drink to put them to sleep. Hard liquor was also commonly used as a medicine, so the fact that people drank, on average, a bottle of whiskey a week is not as surprising or shocking as it might seem on the surface. Then again, that was an average figure, which meant that many men drank far more than a bottle of whiskey a week.

Hence the need in 1826 for the American Temperance Society (ATS), founded, ironically, in Boston, Massachusetts, just forty miles from Plymouth Rock. You know there was a nationwide need for an organization like this by the fact that within five years the ATS had 170,000 members in 2,200 local chapters, and within ten years, it had 1.5 million members, which was more than 10 percent of the population at that time. To put it into perspective, that's about the same percentage of the population that belongs to the Republican Party today.

Initially, the ATS supported a more commonsense approach to the growing drinking problem: its members agreed to give up hard liquor except for medicinal use but still enjoyed beer and wine in moderation. Some did sign a pledge to give up alcohol totally, and in membership records these people were identified by a *T*, for "total," next to their names, hence the word *teetotal*. If everyone had followed the ATS's early example, Prohibition may never have happened, but there were large numbers of people who felt that the only way to solve the problem was to ban alcohol completely. The ATS later became part of the larger movement calling for prohibition, and this itself was part of an even larger movement working for broader reforms in society, such as the abolition of slavery and women's rights.

In 1893 the Anti-Saloon League (ASL) was founded in Ohio, whose mission was to save people from "the evils of the drink habit and . . . the debauching curse of the drink traffic." Like the ATS before it, it very quickly became a national organization. It also quickly made itself the most forceful and important of the many organizations campaigning for Prohibition. It did so by lobbying the politicians who would do the voting, regardless of their personal stances on the issue. ATS organizers knew full well that politicians are capable of saying one thing while doing another, so they didn't try to stop the politicians themselves from drinking; they only cared about whether the politicians would vote to stop other people from drinking, which, on October 28, 1919, they did.

PROHIBITION TIMELINE

The Road to Prohibition

1913: The Sixteenth Amendment is ratified, allowing Congress to levy income taxes without apportioning it among the states. This reduces the government's reliance on alcohol taxes.

1917: The United States enters World War I, and concerns about conserving resources and maintaining wartime discipline contribute to the push for temperance.

1919: The Eighteenth Amendment is ratified, prohibiting the manufacture, sale, and transportation of intoxicating liquors. The Volstead Act is passed to enforce Prohibition, defining what constitutes intoxicating liquors.

Prohibition Era (1920–1933)

1920: Prohibition officially begins, leading to the closure of bars, saloons, and the rise of illegal speakeasies.

1923: President Warren G. Harding commutes the sentences of many Prohibition violators, reflecting growing public dissatisfaction with the policy.

1925: Organized crime syndicates, including figures like Al Capone, exploit the lucrative illegal alcohol trade.

1929: The St. Valentine's Day Massacre, a violent confrontation between rival gangs in Chicago, highlights the brutality associated with the illegal alcohol trade.

1930: The Brookhart-Sheppard Amendment allows the sale of low-alcohol beer, addressing some public demand for alcohol.

Repeal of Prohibition

1932: Franklin D. Roosevelt is elected president, and his platform includes support for the repeal of Prohibition.

1933: The Twenty-First Amendment is ratified, repealing the Eighteenth Amendment and effectively ending Prohibition. This marks the first and only time in US history that an amendment has been repealed.

Post-Prohibition Era

1933: The Twenty-First Amendment is ratified, officially ending Prohibition on December 5. States regain the authority to regulate alcohol within their borders.

1934: The Alcohol Control Administration is established to oversee the regulation of the alcohol industry at the federal level.

1935: The Federal Alcohol Administration Act is enacted, providing further regulation of the alcoholic beverage industry.

The bill enacting Prohibition became known informally as the Volstead Act, after Andrew Volstead. Volstead chaired the House Judiciary Committee, which managed the legislation, which had actually been drafted by Wayne Wheeler, an attorney who led the Anti-Saloon League. The ASL had already been successful at the state level by getting many states to ban alcohol. In some cases, they leveraged World War I, stating that grain should be used for food for the war effort, not for making alcohol, and also that drinking beer was pro-German. Many brewers were indeed of German descent with German names, but the fact that they were themselves as American as apple pie didn't matter.

The War Time Prohibition Act in 1918 merely pushed the door open for the Volstead Act, although there was a powerful figure pushing the door from the other side: President Woodrow Wilson. The president initially vetoed the proposed Volstead Act, but the House voted to override the veto, and then Congress did the same by a vote of 65 to 20, a large enough margin to allow them to veto the veto without further vetoes and open that door to national Prohibition.

Interestingly, although the Volstead Act called for the banning of "intoxicating liquor," it didn't define intoxicating liquor. Some people who voted for the bill took that to mean hard liquor, not beer and wine, but when it came down later to defining intoxicating liquor, it was deemed to be anything that contained more than half a percent of alcohol (or one degree proof). Even today Coors Light is 4.2 percent ABV (8.4 proof). So apart from a virtually alcohol-free beer, beer and wine were both off the menu, too. The moral of this story is: don't vote for something that isn't clearly defined.

What's also curious is that the act banned the making, transporting, and selling of "intoxicating liquor," but not the buying or drinking of it. It seems strange that only the seller is committing a crime in this transaction, when it takes two to tango. And if it's not illegal to buy alcohol nor to drink it, how could the confiscation of liquor that was legally purchased be justified? The act had many gray areas like this, which is unbelievable for something as significant as an amendment to the US Constitution.

Nor did the government set aside sufficient funds to enforce the act, as we saw in chapter 2. Many of the proponents of Prohibition thought that if alcohol were banned, people would simply get out of the habit of drinking, and the United States would be a better place for it. How wrong they were, as Karen Blumenthal writes in *Bootleg: Murder, Moonshine, and the Lawless Years of Prohibition*:

> Prohibition, as it was called, was a grand social revolution that was supposed to forever end drunkenness, reduce crime, and make life better for America's families. Nine years later, the results were quite different. People who had always followed the rules now openly ignored the highest law of the land. Children helped their parents secretly concoct brews. Young people carried flasks of whiskey in their pockets to look fashionable and hung out at illegal "speakeasies," drinking. Teenage boys acted as lookouts for bootleggers or drove cars and boats loaded with illegal liquor to big cities.... Rather than become more moral and upright, America, in the eyes of many, had become a lawless society. How had such good intentions gone so terribly, terribly wrong?

Blumenthal also points out that Prohibition even made lawbreakers of religious communities. People could buy alcohol for medicinal or religious purposes, so Catholic priests were buying "communion wine" by the case and selling it to their congregation. It was too much for one rabbi, though: "'They kept calling for wine, wine, and more wine,' said Rabbi B. Gardner, who saw his synagogue grow from 180 members to nearly 1,200 members in just over a year. 'I refused to violate the law to please them.'"

President Wilson may have failed in his attempt to veto the Volstead Act, but his 1920 successor, President Warren Harding, took another approach and simply ignored it. White House guests continued to enjoy predinner cocktails and wines with their meals. In theory, the city of Washington had been dry since November 1, 1917, when the Sheppard Act banned the sale of alcohol in the District of Columbia. You wouldn't have known that if you visited the White House, where every brand of liquor and fine wine was readily available. Capitol Hill was one of the booziest places in the country, so it was no surprise that much of that country ignored Prohibition too.

A lot of the White House's liquor was provided by a bootlegger named George Cassiday, whose mother was a member of the Women's Christian Temperance Union and whose father was teetotal for the last thirty-two years of his life. Cassiday himself didn't drink much, either, but when Prohibition was approved, he was serving as a soldier in France in the aftermath of World War I and enjoying a little cognac as part of his rations.

When Cassiday returned to the United States in 1919, he failed the physical to return to his job as a brakeman, so he started looking for work. A friend introduced him to two members of Congress from an unnamed southern state who were looking for some liquor. Cassiday found some for these southern gentlemen, both of whom had voted in favor of Prohibition. Soon Cassiday had other customers in both the Senate and House, and a Midwest representative offered to help him get his own room in the House building to use as a base so that he could bring in larger quantities of booze rather than fulfill orders individually as he received them.

In those days, there were no searches of anyone entering the building, only those leaving, so Cassiday walked in carrying suitcases filled with booze. He would lock himself in the room and pull down the blinds, and word soon got round that a special knock on this door signaled the bootlegger to unlock it and do business. He sometimes sat in the gallery to listen to speeches and debates and saw firsthand some of his regular customers praising Prohibition and its enforcement. Not only were these representatives buying liquor for themselves, they were also keeping their staff well stocked, too.

It was 1925 before Cassiday was eventually stopped by a security guard—probably after a tipoff from a "dry" representative—and charged with transporting alcohol in the House building. He was given a ninety-day jail sentence. As stated earlier, it wasn't a crime to buy alcohol, only to make, sell, or transport it. None of Cassiday's customers had committed any crimes. Although he was banned from the House building, after serving his sentence Cassiday was able to find himself a room in the Senate building so that he could resume his activities.

It would be another five years before Cassiday was arrested again, this time as the result of a sting operation in which Cassiday agreed to supply some gin to a new customer, only to find himself arrested by two agents from the Prohibition Bureau. He got jail time again, though on this occasion, he had to report to the jail only during the day and was allowed to spend the nights at home, a sign that being a bootlegger on Capitol Hill wasn't seen as a serious crime.

Cassiday cashed in on his experiences by writing a series of articles for the *Washington Post*, which—without naming names—exposed the hypocrisy at the heart of government. He estimated that he sold liquor to about 80 percent of the senators and congressmen in Washington, DC, as well as to many of their secretaries and other staff. The stories appeared just before the 1930 midterm elections and may well have helped the Democrats, who by then were in favor of repealing Prohibition, to regain control of Congress.

Liquor use didn't stop with the representatives, either. President Harding, as mentioned earlier, ignored Prohibition completely. He liked his whiskey, and he liked his poker, hosting games regularly in his office, where the alcohol flowed freely and First Lady Florence Harding made cocktails for the regulars who became known as the Poker Cabinet. Indeed, FBI records showed that during a 1922 railroad strike, the president was known to be drunk while meeting with the railroad workers' leaders in the Oval Office.

Harding didn't deal directly with bootleggers like Cassiday. He didn't need to. His attorney general, Harry Daugherty, and a colleague named Jess Smith kept the White House supplied. Why pay a bootlegger when the Justice Department provided confiscated stock from the Prohibition Bureau? Smith also used some of the liquor to persuade journalists not to run stories critical of the president, who was a known womanizer as well as a drinker and gambler. Some of the booze also went to keeping his mistresses quiet. Harding died of a heart attack on August 2, 1923, without completing his first term in office.

That same year, Alphonse Gabriel Capone began taking an interest in the politics of the Illinois town of Cicero, now a suburb of the city of Chicago, where Capone had been living since 1919. When he arrived in Chicago, Capone's first job was as a bouncer in a brothel, but before long, he would become the most notorious gangster and bootlegger in the city's history.

In 1923 he was thinking about expanding his Chicago operations into Cicero and moving there himself, which meant taking an interest in local politics and politicians. Would they present problems or would they be amenable to his planned operations, like bootlegging and opening speakeasies and gambling dens? Capone and his brother Frank began by bribing lower level officials but saw that they would have to do something about those at the top. With elections coming up in 1924, it was important that the right people win—Capone's people.

Brother Frank was tasked with finding Capone-friendly candidates for various local government positions or persuading existing candidates that they would become Capone friendly if they knew what was good for them and their families. On Election Day, Capone's mobsters were out in force, making sure that voters knew whom to vote for, and, if they were planning to vote for the wrong people, beating up or otherwise preventing them from voting, even kidnapping them and holding them till the election was over. The situation became so bad that the Cicero police called in the Chicago cops for reinforcements to try to maintain order.

When they arrived, one group of Chicago cops spotted Frank Capone on the street and drove toward him. Frank thought they were rival gangsters and pulled his gun; the police promptly peppered him with bullets, killing him. After that incident, Al Capone never traveled anywhere without a team of bodyguards to protect him. His candidates also "won" the local elections, which was a big step on the road to becoming Chicago's leading gangster.

Capone had been on the wrong side of the law ever since his youth in Brooklyn. He was born in 1899, one of nine children. His parents emigrated from Italy in 1893 and arrived in the United States penniless. His father worked as a barber and his mother as a seamstress, but the respectable hard-working life did not appeal to the teenage Capone. Two of his brothers, Ralph and Frank, would also embrace the criminal lifestyle, whereas brother James would change his name to Richard Hart and become a Prohibition agent in Nebraska. He was clearly the black sheep of the family.

Capone's first serious brush with authority came at the age of fourteen, when he started a fistfight with a female teacher, hit her in the face, and was expelled. He never bothered to find another school and instead picked up casual jobs, working in a candy store and a bowling alley and running messages for a mobster named Johnny Torrio. He played semiprofessional baseball for a while but also worked his way through various street gangs including the Junior Forty Thieves, the Bowery Boys, the Brooklyn Rippers, and the powerful Five Points Gang. Among other members of the Five Points Gang were Lucky Luciano and the man who would later become Capone's mentor and his partner in Chicago, Johnny Torrio.

It was Torrio who first moved to Chicago and later invited Capone to follow him, along with brothers Frank and Ralph. Initially working under the gang leader Big Jim Colosimo, they proved to be a powerful team. Colosimo ran a chain of brothels where Frank and Al both worked and where Al caught syphilis after sampling the goods. He could have been treated, but he didn't want Torrio to know what he'd been up to, and syphilitic dementia tormented him the rest of his life.

When Torrio saw that Prohibition was on the horizon, he began buying breweries with a view to adding bootlegging to the gang's portfolio. Instead, this led to a major falling-out with Colosimo, who was afraid it would draw too much attention to his existing enterprises.

The argument was resolved when Colosimo was shot dead on May 11, 1920, in a café that he owned as one of his legitimate businesses. Torrio and the Capone brothers took over running the gang, known as the Outfit. Although Torrio brought in a hitman from New York to take out Colosimo, it's thought that Capone was also in on the killing.

The empire was therefore extended from prostitution and gambling to include bootlegging, thanks to the newly enacted Prohibition and Torrio's foresight. Capone arranged to get most of his liquor supplies from Canada, where prohibition operated on a province-by-province basis, but there was no national prohibition. After all, the Canadian border was only a little more than three hundred miles from Chicago, with the big city of Toronto another two hundred miles or so beyond that. With the Canada-US border running through four of the five Great Lakes and the difficulties of establishing border checks in the middle of a body of water, the lakes and adjoining rivers proved to be perfect for smuggling liquor into the United States. That was why the White House, and Al Capone for that matter, didn't have to resort to serving moonshine to their guests. No, the world's top brands were just a few hours away.

Things rolled along well for the Outfit during the early years of Prohibition. The gang just grew and grew, business boomed, and they all became very rich from bootleg liquor. Then in 1925, Johnny Torrio was shot several times in an assassination attempt by rival gangsters and seriously injured. He survived but decided to retire, and Al Capone took over as leader of the Outfit. Capone would soon be earning an estimated $100 million a year (about $1.8 billion today), though about $6 million of that went to pay off the police, persuading them to turn a blind eye to his activities.

By this time, Capone was known to be absolutely ruthless, and other gangs tended to keep out of his way. If anyone did cross his path, they were murdered but often tortured first. In 1926, Capone was arrested and charged with three murders, but he spent only one night in jail and was released due to lack of evidence. That was typical. If he was linked to any killings, he could usually prove that he was somewhere else at the time, and few people were foolish enough to offer evidence to the police, who were frequently on Capone's books anyway.

Bootlegging was also behind one of the most notorious killings that Capone was associated with: the St. Valentine's Day Massacre. The seven victims were members or associates of Capone's main rivals, the predominantly Irish North Side Gang, led by George "Bugs" Moran. The killings took place on February 14, 1929, in a warehouse at the center of Moran's bootlegging operations. A lot of Capone's money now came from bootlegging, and he wanted to dominate the business in and around Chicago. Moran had other ideas and was pushing in on Capone's territory. Capone decided to teach him a lesson. Moran also had recently hijacked a boat of Capone's that was bringing in some expensive whiskey from Canada along the Detroit River, a popular smuggling route.

Just before 10:30 a.m., four men arrived in a police car at the bootlegging warehouse at 2122 North Clark Street in Chicago's Lincoln Park neighborhood. Two of them wore police uniforms, and between them they carried two submachine guns and a shotgun. The seven men inside the warehouse would have assumed it was a police raid, not an unusual occurrence when you're in a gang, and complied with orders to get up against the wall. They were ripped apart by the immediate gunfire. The bullet holes are still visible in the wall, which was later dismantled and then rebuilt inside the Mob Museum in Las Vegas.

The two men, who were dressed as cops, then walked out of the building as if arresting the two killers at gunpoint, got back into the police car, and drove off. Among the victims was Moran's second-in-command, who was also his brother-in-law. Moran himself was one of the intended victims but he was absent. Capone was, naturally, a long way from the killings, in his Florida home in Miami Beach. No charges were ever brought.

Capone was now at the peak of his power, but it wouldn't last for much longer. He may well have gotten away with murder, but he couldn't avoid the Internal Revenue Service. The massacre had drawn even more attention to him, and a delegation from the city went to Washington to meet with President Hoover. The meeting was arranged by Walter A. Strong, who published the *Chicago Daily News* and happened to be friendly with the president. Along with him were Frank Loesch of the Chicago Crime Commission and Laird Bell, a prominent Chicago lawyer. They told Hoover that gangsters were taking over Chicago, the gangs were out of control, and federal help was needed to break them up. Hoover agreed.

A concerted effort was made by several government agencies to monitor the gangs' activities and to bring charges against them—any charges. Capone was a particular target. Just six weeks after the massacre, he was arrested when leaving a courtroom where he was giving evidence to a grand jury at an inquiry into Prohibition violations. He was charged with contempt of court for feigning illness in order to avoid a previous court appearance. A few weeks later, he was arrested in Philadelphia for carrying a concealed weapon. He was indicted the next day, pleaded guilty, and was sentenced to a year in prison. The authorities were starting to nip at his ankles and continued to do so.

In April 1930, he was charged with vagrancy in Florida in an attempt to force him to leave the state. The authorities there were doing everything in their power to get Capone out of their hair, and he and his lawyers were doing everything they could to deny them that pleasure. A judge had even ruled that some of the state's tactics were illegal, but that didn't stop them. On May 8, 1930, Capone, his brother John, and two other men, including Capone's bodyguard, were arrested for "investigation." The following day they were released, but Capone had been told that he would continue to face such harassment every time he set foot in Miami Beach.

The authorities were coming after him from a different angle: through income tax. In 1927 the Supreme Court had ruled that illegal income, such as bootlegging or prostitution, was still a person's income and therefore subject to income tax. Capone was clearly a wealthy man, as his lifestyle showed, yet he paid no income tax. Capone's brother Ralph had already been convicted of tax evasion and spent eighteen months in prison. Capone offered to pay taxes but provided ludicrously low figures for his claimed income, such as $100,000 for both 1928 and 1929, probably about 10 percent of his actual earnings.

Capone would have done well to come clean and pay up or to make a deal, but in 1931 his refusal brought his downfall. On March 13 he was charged with tax evasion for 1924. On June 5, the years 1925 through 1929 were added to the charges, along with five thousand violations of the

Volstead Act, and Capone was freed on $50,000 bail. Not for long, though. On June 16 he pleaded guilty as part of a plea deal agreement. However, on July 30, the judge reneged on the plea deal so Capone withdrew his admission of guilt. On October 17 he was found guilty on five charges of tax evasion, and a week later he received an eleven-year sentence.

He began his sentence in Atlanta in May 1932 and in August 1934 was transferred to a new high-security prison in San Francisco: Alcatraz. Here his syphilitic dementia worsened, to the extent that it spread into his brain and he became virtually incoherent. He spent the last year of his sentence in the prison hospital, and when his sentence was completed at Alcatraz, he was transferred to the prison at Terminal Island in San Pedro, California, to complete his sentence on the earlier contempt of court charges. His wife appealed for clemency on the grounds of his impaired mental state, and he was pardoned on November 16, 1939. He died on January 25, 1947, after suffering a stroke and then a heart attack.

Another bootlegger who was once on top of the world but came to a sad end was George Remus, whose bootleg empire was said to have been even bigger than Capone's. That was possible because he dealt only in bootlegging, unlike Capone, who had a larger criminal network that included gambling, prostitution, embezzlement, robberies, and more.

Capone had a conventional route into crime, through the street gangs of New York. Remus had a decidedly more unusual pathway; he first trained as a pharmacist and then switched careers to become a successful lawyer before moving on to bootlegging. He was said to have been one of the models for the character Jay Gatsby in *The Great Gatsby*, and Remus ended up murdering his wife. Like Capone, he got away with murder in an extremely unusual manner.

Remus was born in Germany in 1878 and moved with his parents to the United States in 1882, winding up in Chicago. Several more children were born, but his father struggled to find work. George became the breadwinner at the age of fourteen when he began working in his uncle's pharmacy. Whereas Al Capone was streetwise but not intellectual, Remus was smart and easily could have had a successful legitimate career. He was also an industrious and ambitious young man, and within five years, he had graduated from the Chicago College of Pharmacy. Being a qualified pharmacist would prove useful during Prohibition, as it meant that he was legally entitled to buy alcohol for medicinal purposes and to dispense prescriptions for customers, enabling them to buy alcohol for themselves—for medicinal purposes only, of course.

Two years after graduating, he bought his first pharmacy. Then he bought another one. He grew tired of running the stores himself, though, and decided to leave their management to his staff and become a lawyer instead. Attending the Illinois College of Law, he specialized in criminal defense, particularly for murder cases, and in one notable case in 1914, he used a new defense technique known as "transitory insanity." Now known as "temporary insanity," this defense became useful when, thirteen years later, he himself would be charged for the murder of his wife.

Meanwhile, yet another career move beckoned. Although he was a successful lawyer, he noticed that some of the clients he defended on bootlegging charges made far more money than he did. He was still a qualified pharmacist and still owned his pharmacies, so after a careful lawyer-like study of the Volstead Act, he began buying distilleries for their stocks of alcohol, which he would ostensibly use for medicinal purposes. He then bought even more pharmacies so that he could expand the business. This was perfectly legal. What wasn't legal was that the legal medicinal whiskey deliveries were being hijacked by other people employed by Remus in his burgeoning bootleg business, so that the liquor could make its way into the much more lucrative black market.

Around the time that Al Capone moved into Chicago, George Remus moved out. He moved to Cincinnati in order to be closer to places like Louisville and Lexington and the numerous Kentucky distilleries that closed because of Prohibition, leaving them with large stocks of maturing, famous-name whiskeys and bourbons. These names were much too good to be wasted on medicinal use. Distribution became much easier and quicker and therefore more profitable. Remus was soon making millions of dollars a year.

His wealth—and his showmanship—were on display at the lavish parties that he hosted, including one notable example. On New Year's Eve 1921, when Prohibition was barely two years old, Remus wanted to celebrate the opening of a swimming pool at the mansion that he and his wife Imogene had had built. More than one hundred people were invited, and journalists, judges, and politicians mingled with some of Remus's trusted employees—presumably trusted to never honestly answer the question, "What do you do for a living?" The politicians and journalists were probably trusted not to ask the question in the first place nor to inquire about the origins of the vast amounts of rare wine and liquor available. Not that Remus drank any, as he was teetotal.

While guests chatted before dinner, they were served hors d'oeuvres from solid silver plates, and Remus lit cigars with hundred-dollar bills. When they sat down for dinner, each guest found a thousand-dollar bill underneath his or her plate, equivalent to about $18,000 today. Times one hundred guests. Each of the men then received a jewelry box that contained an inscribed gold watch and a diamond-studded stickpin. The women received a set of car keys, and when they left at the end of the evening, they found fifty expensive cars lined up in the driveway.

As the clock ticked toward midnight, Remus invited everyone to admire his new swimming pool. In the pool, a synchronized swimming team entertained the guests to music from a live orchestra. The New Year began with most of the guests in the pool, including Remus and the members of the orchestra, still in their tuxes.

In 1925 Remus's luck ran out, and he was charged with thousands of breaches of the Volstead Act. He was sentenced to two years in prison and served his time in the Atlanta Federal Penitentiary. This is where his troubles really began. He told a fellow inmate that no one could touch his money because everything, including their mansion, was in Imogene's name. Unfortunately, the prisoner wasn't a real inmate, but an undercover Prohibition agent named Franklin Dodge, who was gathering incriminating information from prisoners.

Dodge decided to look after number one, and while Remus was still in jail in Atlanta, he sought out Imogene and began an affair with her. The two of them cleaned Remus out, taking his money, removing precious artworks and expensive furniture from the mansion, locking Remus out, and selling one of his distilleries—but giving Remus only $100 from the proceeds. When Remus next saw his beloved swimming pool—by breaking into the grounds—it was empty, as was the mansion. The couple had even taken one of his prized personal possessions: a document with George Washington's signature. Remus was understandably mad, as in angry, but did this help turn him mad, as in insane?

Imogene and Dodge attempted to hire a gunman to take care of Remus, who was not taking things quietly. Instead of accepting their money, though, the gunman told Remus about the couple's plans, which dashed any lingering hopes of regaining Imogene's favors. In 1927 Imogene filed for divorce, which was to be finalized at the courthouse in Cincinnati on October 6.

On his way to the courthouse, Remus spotted Imogene and her daughter in a cab, headed in the same direction. He ordered his driver to follow them, chasing them into Eden Park and eventually forcing them off the road. Imogene got out of the cab. Remus jumped out of his car and fatally shot her in the stomach in front of horrified park visitors.

When his trial came to court, Remus opted to defend himself and turned to his past experiences—and showmanship—as a criminal defense lawyer. He used the "transitory insanity" defense, which had worked in 1914, and pulled out all the stops in a bravura display (including a histrionic breakdown), casting himself as the wronged man who was indeed temporarily insane when he pulled the trigger. The jury took all of nineteen minutes to find him innocent, but because the verdict said that he was insane, he was committed to an insane asylum.

In fact, the whole situation became quite insane itself, in a catch-22 kind of way. Remus was examined by various psychiatrists who couldn't decide whether he was sane or insane—and if he was insane, whether it was temporary or permanent—or whether he was simply playacting. Remus demanded to be released, now saying that because the prosecution, with the help of three psychiatrists, had declared him sane and therefore fit to stand trial for murder, he didn't belong in an asylum. He was released after seven months, and because of a double-jeopardy ruling, he couldn't be charged for the same offense twice.

After his release, Remus didn't resume his illegal activities but instead chose to live a quiet life in Covington, Kentucky, just across the river from Cincinnati. He eventually married his longtime secretary and ran a small contracting company until he had a stroke and passed away from a cerebral hemorrhage in 1952 at the age of seventy-three.

Not all Prohibition bootleggers were immigrants, though the most successful ones, like George Remus and Al Capone, were. So too was Rocco Perri, who became the biggest bootlegger in Canada and was sometimes described as the Canadian Al Capone. Before delving into the interesting life and times of Rocco Perri, it's worth trying to untangle the complicated history of prohibition in Canada.

Just as in the United States, there were movements toward prohibition in Canada in the nineteenth century. Extreme drunkenness was a problem there, too, leading to the founding of various temperance organizations. The Canada Temperance Act of 1864 allowed any city or county within the Province of Canada (then a British colony) to ban the sale of alcohol, provided a majority of citizens voted in favor. In 1877, the Province of Canada was dissolved, leading to the start of the formation of modern Canada.

In 1878, the Canada Temperance Act extended the optional ban on the sale of alcohol to the four provinces that made up the new Canadian Confederation. This act stayed in effect until 1964. Many cities and counties did opt in to prohibition, and a national referendum was called in 1898, the same year the Yukon Territory was created. The call for a national ban on alcohol was passed by a 51 percent majority, but voter turnout was a very low 44 percent, and one province, Quebec, voted 80 percent against prohibition. Because of these last two factors, the government decided not to implement national prohibition, since it was felt that the vote wasn't clear-cut and it would be too divisive.

Most provinces introduced prohibition during World War I, and national prohibition came into effect on April 1, 1918. This made it illegal to import alcohol stronger than 2.5 percent ABV, which ruled out all wine, spirits, and anything but the very weakest of beers. The making of alcohol was also now banned, except for medicinal and religious use, and inter-province trading in alcohol was also illegal. This was the opportunity that would turn Rocco Perri from a small-time criminal and occasional dealer in illicit booze into an international bootlegger and a very rich man.

Perri had been born in 1887 in Italy's Calabria region, one of the poorest parts of the country. His parents were shepherds, and so among the poorest of the poor. Perri and his friends saw the United States as the land of opportunity, and Perri decided to seize that opportunity and immigrated to the United States at the age of sixteen, leaving his family behind. He got a job as a laborer but five years later in 1908 decided to move to Canada to find work.

FAMOUS TEMPERANCE SUPPORTERS

Leo Tolstoy

The Russian author of such momentous works as *War and Peace* and *Anna Karenina* abstained from alcohol and tobacco. He believed both substances were harmful and would prevent people from leading productive and virtuous lives. In *Anna Karenina*, Tolstoy depicted the negative consequences of alcoholism through the character of Konstantin Levin, who struggles with alcohol abuse and its impact on his life and relationships. This portrayal reflects Tolstoy's awareness of the destructive effects of alcohol on individuals and families.

Vladimir Lenin

The czars of Russia ruled through vodka. They held a monopoly on vodka supplies, which could be acquired only through state-owned bars. The serfs remained subjugated because of their love of vodka, and the czars' lifestyle and the country's economy were supported by the cash that vodka brought into the coffers.

Things changed after Lenin became the founding head of the Soviet government in 1917. He and his fellow Bolsheviks supported temperance efforts as part of their broader social and political aims. During the early years of Soviet rule, the government implemented policies aimed at reducing alcohol consumption. These measures included restrictions on alcohol production, distribution, and sales, as well as campaigns promoting sobriety and productivity. Lenin himself expressed support for temperance initiatives, seeing them as aligned with the goals of building a more productive and disciplined society. He believed that excessive drinking undermined the revolutionary spirit and hindered efforts to build socialism.

Lenin and the Soviet government eventually moderated their stance on temperance. In the later years of Lenin's leadership and especially under Stalin's rule, the Soviet Union

relaxed its anti-alcohol policies to some extent, acknowl-
edging the difficulties in achieving total sobriety through pro-
hibition-style measures.

Mahatma Gandhi

Mahatma Gandhi, the influential leader of India's independence movement, had a significant connection with the temperance movement. Gandhi advocated for temperance as part
of his broader philosophy of nonviolence, social reform, and
personal morality. He believed that alcohol consumption was
detrimental to individual well-being and societal progress. He
saw alcohol as a tool of exploitation by colonial powers and a
barrier to India's development and self-reliance. Gandhi also
linked alcohol abuse to poverty, violence, and social injustice.

Throughout his life, Gandhi actively promoted temperance
through various means. He encouraged his followers to abstain from alcohol and other intoxicants, emphasizing the importance of self-discipline and moral purity. Gandhi himself
was a teetotaler, abstaining from alcohol and tobacco.

Abraham Lincoln

Lincoln was known for moderation in his personal habits,
including alcohol consumption. He wasn't a heavy drinker
and abstained from alcohol for extended periods, particularly during his presidency. Although there's no evidence that
Lincoln publicly advocated for temperance or supported prohibition, his personal example of moderation likely resonated
with temperance advocates.

During Lincoln's presidency, the issue of alcohol consumption intersected with broader social and political concerns,
particularly during the Civil War. Some temperance advocates
argued that alcohol abuse among soldiers was detrimental to
military discipline and effectiveness. As a result, there were
efforts within the Union Army to promote temperance and dis-
courage excessive drinking among soldiers. Although Lincoln
did not initiate these efforts himself, he was aware of the

issues surrounding alcohol abuse in the military and supported measures to maintain discipline and morale among
Union troops.

Thomas Jefferson

Jefferson is known for his promotion of personal liberty and
limited government intervention in individuals' lives, which
might suggest a reluctance to support measures such as
prohibition advocated by some temperance groups. However,
he also expressed concerns about excessive alcohol consumption and its potential negative effects on society.

In a letter to Thomas Cooper in 1811, Jefferson wrote
about his observations of the effects of alcohol, expressing
concern about its abuse among some members of society.
He stated, "I am heartily an advocate for some restriction of
the elective franchise," suggesting that he believed certain
individuals should not have access to alcohol due to its detrimental effects on their behavior.

Frederick Douglass

Frederick Douglass, the prominent abolitionist, social re-
former, and writer, had a notable connection with the temperance movement during his lifetime. Douglass was deeply
committed to various social reform causes beyond the abolition of slavery, including women's rights, education, and
temperance.

Douglass recognized the detrimental effects of alcohol
abuse on individuals and communities, particularly within
African American communities. He witnessed firsthand the
impact of alcoholism on families and the struggle for self-
improvement and advancement among African Americans.
He believed that temperance was essential for the moral
and social upliftment of society, particularly for marginalized
groups seeking to overcome oppression and achieve equality.
He saw alcoholism as a form of bondage that perpetuated cy-
cles of poverty and dependency.

Throughout his life, Douglass actively supported temperance initiatives and worked alongside temperance advocates to promote sobriety and moral reform. He delivered speeches, wrote articles, and used his platform to raise awareness about the dangers of alcohol abuse and the importance of temperance. In his newspaper, the *North Star*, and other publications, Douglass often addressed issues related to temperance and advocated for personal responsibility, self-discipline, and moral virtue. He encouraged individuals to abstain from alcohol and embrace sober living as a means of improving their lives and contributing to the betterment of society.

"Pussyfoot" Johnson

"Pussyfoot" Johnson, whose full name was William E. Johnson, was a colorful figure in the temperance movement in the United States during the late nineteenth and early twentieth centuries. He earned his nickname due to his stealthy and persistent efforts in enforcing prohibition laws, particularly in the Midwest. He was born in Illinois in 1862 and became involved in the temperance movement in early adulthood.

He gained notoriety for his confrontational and sometimes theatrical methods of advocating for temperance and enforcing prohibition laws. Johnson often dressed in disguise and conducted raids on saloons and bars suspected of serving alcohol illegally. One of Johnson's most famous actions was the "Chain Gang," a group of men he organized to destroy saloons in Kansas in 1901. He also participated in various other raids and protests aimed at shutting down establishments that violated Prohibition laws.

Despite his zealous efforts, Johnson was not universally praised. Critics accused him of vigilantism and excessive zeal in enforcing temperance laws. However, he remained undeterred in his mission to promote sobriety and curb alcohol consumption. Johnson's activities coincided with the broader temperance movement's push for prohibition laws, which eventually culminated in the passage of the Volstead Act, prohibiting the manufacture, sale, and transportation of alcoholic beverages.

After the federal enactment of Prohibition, Johnson continued his advocacy work, although with less visibility. However, with the eventual repeal of Prohibition in 1933, his activities in the temperance movement gradually faded into obscurity.

Carrie Nation

Carrie A. Nation was a prominent figure in the temperance and prohibition movements, and probably the most notorious. She was known for her aggressive and unconventional tactics in advocating for temperance and the prohibition of alcohol. Born Carrie Amelia Moore in 1846, Carrie Nation became involved in the temperance movement after experiencing personal hardships related to her first husband's alcoholism. She believed that alcohol was the root cause of many social problems, including poverty, violence, and family breakdown.

She gained national attention for her "hatchetations," which involved using a hatchet or a similar tool to smash saloon fixtures and alcohol bottles. Her actions were often accompanied by prayers and hymn singing, as she believed she was doing God's work by destroying places that sold alcohol. Nation's radical methods earned her both admirers and detractors. Some saw her as a crusader for morality and public health, while others criticized her for her confrontational approach and questioned the legality of her actions.

Despite facing arrests and legal challenges, Carrie Nation remained committed to her cause and continued her crusade against alcohol until her death in 1911. Her activism played a role in shaping public opinion and contributing to the eventual passage of prohibition laws in the United States, including the Eighteenth Amendment to the Constitution.

In Canada, Perri again worked for a while as a laborer in the construction industry, and for a time worked in a bakery and as a macaroni salesman. However, he was getting involved in petty crime on the side, including a bit of illicit buying and selling of whatever was wanted. When the Ontario Temperance Act became law in 1916, he and his common-law wife, Bessie Starkman, an immigrant from Poland, saw an opportunity for a specific type of illicit buying and selling. The act allowed for the continued production of alcohol for export purposes and for the import of alcohol for medicinal and religious use. As George Remus had found in Cincinnati, there were legal loopholes big enough to pass a crate of whiskey through.

The couple was living reasonably comfortably at the time on Perri's regular income from selling macaroni. They even managed to open a grocery store. It was here where Perri's bootlegging empire began. They began selling shots of whisky to anyone who knew enough to ask for it. From such small beginnings grew the empire of Canada's biggest bootlegger.

Perri and Starkman (his partner in crime) were living in Hamilton, Ontario, where they also operated brothels. In 1917 Starkman was arrested and fined $50 for keeping a bawdy house after police raided their home and found a prostitute doing what prostitutes do. Although Perri's name has gone down in history, Starkman was a huge part of the story, and it was she who suggested bootlegging in the first place and helped him to run the operation.

That operation began at a time when prohibition was in effect in Ontario but did not exist in Quebec. The pair therefore began smuggling liquor from Montreal into Ontario. When Quebec adopted prohibition in 1919, Perri and Starkman began smuggling booze in from the United States. By the time prohibition arrived in the United States in 1920, statewide prohibition in Quebec had come to an end; after public protests, the banning of alcohol was left for each county to decide for itself. Fortunately for Perri and Starkman, there were enough "wet" counties for them to reverse the rivers of whiskey and get them flowing from Canada into the United States. They even provided Canadian liquor to Al Capone's Chicago Outfit as well as to some notorious gangs in New York.

Perri quickly justified his title as the Canadian Al Capone, becoming the biggest gangster in the country. He and Starkman had expanded beyond bootlegging and prostitution into gambling and extortion. They were also suspected of being involved in the narcotics trade as early as 1922, and by 1924, they were said to be making around Can$1 million a year. Among their customers were governors, senators, judges, and wine-buying clergymen. The entire police force in Hamilton was reputed to be on the payroll. Until this time, the only charges brought against Perri were minor compared to the scale of his operations: leaving the scene of an accident, lying to a police officer, and allowing a ferocious dog to be at large were among them.

Then in 1926 a more serious charge caught up to him. Perri faced criminal charges in the deaths of seventeen people who had died after consuming tainted alcohol that Perri had sold to them. As mentioned before, cheap bootleg liquor may contain all manner of poisonous substances if the distillers were either careless or trying to produce liquor as quickly and as cheaply as possible. Spirits were found to contain sulfuric acid, formaldehyde, and even creosote. However, on January 1, 1927, Perri was found innocent on the grounds that it could not be proved that he knew the alcohol was poisonous. Ironically, it was the same date that alcohol was legalized in Ontario again, although it didn't hamper Perri much, since the rules about consuming it were still very restrictive, with bars and liquor stores having to close early.

Much of Perri's life was shrouded in mystery as he naturally endeavored to keep a low profile, but two major events served to add to the mystery. On August 13, 1930, Bessie Starkman, Perri's partner and the most notorious female gangster in Canadian history, was murdered as she got out of Perri's car in the garage of their home. Two shotgun blasts killed her outright. Perri heard the blasts and chased the gunmen's car down the street but to no avail. He offered a reward for information about her death, but even though he was the most powerful man around, the killers were never tracked down. When she was buried, Perri fainted at her graveside.

The other great mystery in Perri's life occurred in 1944: the disappearance of Rocco Perri. In 1940, Perri and his brother Mike were arrested. Not for bootlegging or any other crime, though. The two were arrested because they were Italians suspected of having connections to Mussolini's fascist regime in Italy, which had sided with Hitler's Germany. By the time Perri was released three years later, other gangsters had taken over his criminal empire and he was unable to step back into his role.

Perri was released in October 1943, and six months later he simply disappeared. There are conflicting accounts about what happened on that fateful day, April 23, 1944. One states that he went to work, but late in the morning he said that he had a headache and went for a walk to clear his head, never to be seen again. Other accounts suggest that he had been at home or at a meeting rather than at work. Whatever the case, all agree that Perri had a headache and went for a walk, only to disappear.

And that was it. He was never seen again. It's highly possible he was killed by rival gangsters either over past deeds or to ensure he did not attempt a comeback, which he'd started to think about doing. An attempt at a suicide note was found in his car but it was clearly not written by Perri, which points the finger at a gangland killing. In 1954, he was officially declared dead, and the Royal Canadian Mountain Police concluded that they would never find his body until Burlington Bay dries up. As yet, that hasn't happened.

Some people in the next chapter disappear, too, some of them after simply walking into a liquor store and walking out again with thousands of dollars' worth of scotch.

· 5 ·

A Guy Walks
into a Liquor Store

It's a classic movie story. A bunch of thieves come out of retirement to commit one last crime. It's going to be the heist of all heists. Except they make one fatal mistake that leads to them being tracked down and captured. In real life, it's more likely to be a small-scale human story in which a petty thief walks into a liquor store, grabs the first bottle of hooch he sees, and makes a run for it, only to be identified when crystal-clear security footage is broadcast all over the local evening news.

However, one guy in Toronto refined this method when he walked into a liquor store and managed to take a rare bottle of fifty-year-old Glenfiddich single malt from a cabinet of rare and vintage whiskies. He then picked up a bottle of cheap wine and calmly walked to the counter. He paid for the wine he'd picked up after concealing the Glenfiddich in his trench coat and draping it over his shoulder like Joe Cool. He earned the smirk he flashed at the security camera as he walked out.

The bold crime happened just before 2:00 p.m. on Sunday, April 7, 2013, at the waterfront Liquor Control Board of Ontario (LCBO) store located at 2 Cooper Street and Queens Quay. It's not known whether the man managed to pick the cabinet's lock or if, to the thief's good fortune, a member of staff accidentally left it unlocked on the very day the thief had planned his visit. Or was there a little inside help? No one will ever know. The theft wasn't even noticed till the following day.

What happened to the counter staff afterward is not recorded, though the LCBO did say, not surprisingly, that it had subsequently reviewed its display practices for more expensive spirits. If any of the staff had their pay docked, it would certainly have stung; the bottle, one of only fifty released worldwide, carried a price tag of $26,000. No doubt the thief toasted his brazen success by opening the cheap bottle of wine afterward. The whiskey was probably saved as an investment or had been stolen to order for a collector.

Police issued a thorough description of the suspect as well as the security camera photo. He was white, around five feet, ten inches, and between thirty-five to forty years old—at least ten years younger than the whiskey. He was clean-shaven, wearing black framed glasses, and last seen wearing black jeans, a plaid Burberry shirt, a brown hat, and carrying a brown trench coat. Glenfiddich issued an equally thorough description of the whiskey as being "pale gold . . . [with] a beautifully harmonious, uplifting, vibrant and complex aroma . . . with a touch of dry oak and the merest trace of peat [on the finish]." Despite such rich details, neither man nor whiskey has been tracked down.

The LCBO had been created in 1927 as a way of easing the restrictions of prohibition, which had been introduced in Canada in 1916. Although national prohibition ceased in 1920, individual provinces were slower to act. Ontario ended prohibition in 1927, and Prince Edward Island not until 1947. The LCBO still operates almost seven hundred stores today and remains one of the world's largest buyers of alcoholic beverages.

Given the state monopoly on alcohol, perhaps it's not surprising that Canadians have developed a habit of stealing their liquor. A less subtle case than the Toronto heist happened in Montreal in January 2015. There, another guy walked into another LCBO liquor store mid-morning and threatened staff and customers with a handgun that may or may not have been real. He helped himself to the most expensive bottle of whiskey on the shelves, a 1962 Balvenie, of which only eighty-eighty bottles were ever produced. The one that was stolen was the only bottle left in all of Canada and worth a cool US$50,000. The thief took a few cheaper bottles for good measure (presumably to drink) and walked off into the streets, never to be apprehended.

Most whiskey thieves know what they're after. A bottle of Bowmore single malt worth nearly $12,000 (almost $22,000 today) disappeared from an Edmonton (Canada again) liquor store in 1999. The Islay whiskey had been distilled in 1955, but the single cask was only discovered at the distillery forty years later. A cask might seem a large thing to lose, but it does happen when distilleries may have tens of thousands of them, and they get moved around to other warehouses from time to time. This particular cask produced a mere 294 bottles, making it a collector's item. The person who "collected" this bottle was never found, despite leaving a blood sample behind when he broke into the store to steal the scotch.

That particular whiskey enthusiast got thirsty in the early hours of New Year's Eve 1999, smashing his way into the store on Jasper Avenue in downtown Edmonton. He knew exactly what he wanted: despite the temptations of thousands of bottles of spirits, wines, and beers, including expensive French cognacs, he took only the one bottle of Bowmore. However, he did neglect to take the bottle's certificate of authenticity.

The thief may therefore have found it hard to dispose of, or perhaps he planned to hold it to ransom, since the store owner later received a mysterious phone call offering to reveal the bottle's whereabouts for $4,000. The caller said that more than one thief was involved and that they had been hired specifically to steal that bottle. The owner declined the offer, though by then, he had taken the precaution of placing a different rare bottle of Bowmore that he owned under lock and key and hiding it from public view. The distillery offered an all-expenses-paid trip from Canada to Islay for information leading to the safe recovery of the bottle, though the reward was never claimed. The offer's still available, by the way.

Most booze bandits go after rare whiskeys or fine wines, because the rewards are greater, but beer gets targeted too. In Atlanta in June 2016, thieves got away with more than 78,500 bottles of beer from the SweetWater Brewing Company. The 3,272 cases of SweetWater's summer variety pack were in two refrigerated trailers that had been loaded by the overnight shift for delivery in the morning. Somewhere between 4:00 a.m. and 9:00 a.m., they disappeared.

SWEETWATER BREWING COMPANY

SweetWater Brewing Company was founded in 1997 in Atlanta, Georgia, by Freddy Bensch and Kevin McNerney, who shared a passion for brewing and a love for the outdoors. They began brewing beer in a small warehouse and quickly gained popularity among local beer enthusiasts. Over the years, SweetWater expanded its production capacity and distribution network, reaching customers across the southeastern United States and beyond.

Over the years, SweetWater has experienced significant growth and expansion, both in terms of production capacity and market presence. In 2020, the company announced its acquisition by Canadian cannabis company Aphria Inc. (now Tilray Inc.), as part of Aphria's strategy to diversify its business into the cannabis-infused beverage market while leveraging SweetWater's expertise in brewing and brand recognition.

Once the theft was discovered, the trucks were tracked using their GPS systems. By the time police found them at 3:00 p.m., they were both empty. At 5:00 p.m., after using the GPS history to trace the trucks' routes, police found a quarter of the stolen haul in a warehouse. The owner of the warehouse said he had no idea the beer was stolen. Two guys asked him to store it for them overnight and said they'd collect it the next day. That was the good news for SweetWater. The bad news was that the company had to dispose of the beer in case it had become contaminated while out of its possession.

The following day, SweetWater received a tipoff that someone was trying to sell some of its beer on the street. The police got surveillance footage of the person trying to sell the beer out of his truck. The next day, SweetWater hired a private investigator who worked in conjunction with the Atlanta Police Department, the Southeastern Transportation

Security Council, and the Georgia Bureau of Investigations Major Theft Unit. Among them, it took only twenty-four hours to locate the rest of the stolen beer. That too had to be disposed of. It was sent to a company that would distill it to produce biofuel. SweetWater estimated the stolen beer had a retail value of about $90,000 and would take them two weeks to rebrew that much beer.

One bottle of beer might not be worth much, but steal enough of it and it adds up. For a gang in the Bronx, it added up to $100,000 before they got caught. It happened at a Budweiser warehouse from 2012 to 2013, when staff started noticing discrepancies in the inventories. They began reviewing overnight security footage only to find that on certain nights someone turned the cameras away from the action. They also discovered that on those particular nights, the same security guard, Charles Dandrea, was on duty.

Budweiser contacted the New York Police Department's Forty-First Precinct, which set up a surveillance post the next time Dandrea was working. At 1:15 a.m., they watched while a U-Haul van arrived at the warehouse and five people began loading cases of beer. Dandrea was completely unaware that he had been observed turning the security camera angle away from the robbery this time. Police arrested Dandrea along with the three men and two women in the U-Haul. They also found six bags of marijuana in the van.

Budweiser was also a victim in one of the biggest beer thefts in history, which took place in Dublin, Ireland, in 2007, and involved 39,600 pints of beer. The theft wasn't from any old warehouse but from the Guinness Brewery on Victoria Quay. A man drove into the brewery in a truck, hitched it to a trailer containing 180 kegs of Guinness, 180 kegs of Budweiser, and 90 kegs of Carlsberg, and exited through the security gate and into the city traffic. Guinness brews both Budweiser and Carlsberg in Dublin to sell in Ireland under license. With a retail value of roughly $235,000, the theft from the brewery was the largest since it was founded in Dublin in 1759. If it sounds audacious, it was, but bear in mind that at the time of the robbery, up to 250 trucks were going in and out of the warehouse every day. Two men were arrested and charged with handling stolen goods, and some of the beer was recovered, but the driver was never found.

Down in Austin, Texas, in 2016, twenty-two-year-old Achilles Salazar, who worked at the Capital Beverage Distribution Company, managed to steal at least nine hundred twelve-packs of Dos Equis, Modelo, and other beers during a period of less than a month, amounting to about $90,000 in all. His job was to stack beer onto pallets, which other workers then moved around the warehouse. Salazar's bosses started getting suspicious when they noticed him arriving as much as two hours early and taking it upon himself to drive a forklift and move pallets around.

Other workers got even more suspicious when Salazar moved three pallets of Dos Equis to a loading area when no pickups were scheduled. Salazar was fired and the robberies stopped, but police were later brought in when the extent of the thefts became known. They arrested two people who had bought the stolen beer, recovering 719 cases of Dos Equis from their home (along with $100,000 in cash, a large marijuana plant, and twenty firearms, one of which was a prohibited weapon and two of which were stolen). The two men said they bought the beer from someone answering to Salazar's description, though Salazar himself was never found.

Not everyone gets away with it, though. One Kenneth McLean of Avonbridge near Falkirk in Scotland, halfway between Glasgow and Edinburgh, was found with almost £40,000 ($48,000) of stolen whiskey in his attic. Police received a tipoff about the booze, which turned out to be fifty-seven bottles that had been stolen from a warehouse owned by the giant drink corporation, Diageo. The warehouse was in Grangemouth, eight miles (13 km) from Avonbridge, and had been broken into in July 2016. The haul included nine bottles of a thirty-seven-year-old Port Ellen, worth £2,500 ($3,000) each, and seven bottles of Brora worth £1,750 ($2,100) each.

When the police questioned him about the bottles, McLean claimed that he had purchased them in cash from an unknown person and planned to sell them in several years, once their value appreciated. Duty hadn't been paid on the bottles, though, so it was illegal to buy and sell them in any case. McLean later told a different story to social workers who were reviewing the case: he claimed that he had accepted them in lieu of rent of £1,400 ($1,700) owed to him by one of his tenants. No doubt they tried to keep a straight face when McLean also told them that he had no idea they were stolen. He was sentenced to two hundred hours of community service for possession of stolen goods. Although McLean didn't get away with it, the original thieves were never apprehended.

Neither was the gang that broke into the gift shop at the Glenglassaugh Distillery in Aberdeenshire, Scotland, in June 2014. The crime occurred after 4:30 p.m. on Tuesday, June 10, when the gift shop closed for the day, and 9:30 a.m. on Wednesday, June 11, when it re-opened and staff found the place ransacked.

The thieves took more than £10,000 ($12,000) in goods, including a thirty-seven-year-old Glenglassaugh worth £372 ($445) and a forty-year-old worth £1,200 ($1,435). To make things worse, the thieves also helped themselves to some of the branded merchandise for sale, including sweaters. Walking round proudly advertising a brand of whiskey whose premises you've recently broken into really does add insult to injury. The thieves also stole four pot stills, presumably to sell rather than to start their own distillery.

Not all spirits heists are carried out by thieves who know what they want. Four guys walked into a branch of Total Wine in New Jersey in 2017, and although they walked out with around $52,000 in high-end whiskeys, they also left behind a $42,000 bottle that was in the same cabinet.

When they entered the store, the men took two shopping carts, but they didn't browse the shelves like regular shoppers. The carts were used to block the views of other shoppers while one of the robbers popped open the locked case and helped himself to a Tullibardine 1952 ($28,000), a fifty-year-old Highland Park ($22,000), and a bottle of The Macallan V5 Reflexion (a mere $1,900). Perhaps for a laugh he also took a more modest $68 whiskey called Pinch Scotch. The thieves put the bottles into a white bag and calmly walked out, leaving Total Wine to review its security procedures. The missing whiskey and unlocked cabinet weren't even noticed till the following day.

The men were never caught but police believe they were part of a Chilean criminal gang that carried out a series of robberies of all kinds of expensive goods, not just whiskey. The guy who forced open the cabinet left behind some fingerprints. From these, the police issued a warrant for the arrest of Angel Hernandez Silva. Unfortunately, that was only one of at least four names he used. The man showed up in Texas, where he was arrested for shoplifting a $2,400 purse, but under a different name, Bryan Gonzalez, and using a Puerto Rican driver's license. He was released on bail before the Texas police saw the warrant from New Jersey. He was never seen again.

The South African gang who hijacked a truck filled with about $240,000 worth of Jack Daniel's weren't quite so lucky, or so devious, though they were a bit more subtle. In 2018 in the town of Vereeniging, about an hour south of Johannesburg, six robbers kitted out two cars with flashing blue lights and pulled over the truck. The driver was taken away in one of the cars and released. The police quickly traced the truck to someone's backyard and arrested three of the robbers who were busily unloading the booze. The other three, who had already left with about half the whiskey in another truck, were subsequently arrested when they tried the flashing-blue-lights trick on someone else. The Jack Daniel's seems to have disappeared, though.

One of the most famous names in the whiskey world is Pappy Van Winkle, the whiskey made at the Buffalo Trace Distillery, which definitely has cachet. Thieves are usually more interested in cash than cachet, however, and a bunch of them managed to relieve the distillery of an estimated $100,000 worth of Pappy Van Winkle in a crime that inevitably became known as Pappygate. It was turned into "The Bourbon King," two episodes in Netflix's true-crime series, *Heist*.

The crime was discovered in 2013 when employees checking inventory at Buffalo Trace realized that two hundred bottles of Pappy Van Winkle were missing along with, amazingly, a stainless steel storage barrel of Buffalo Trace's own seventeen-year-old Eagle Rare. A single bottle currently retails for around $2,700, so it was a considerable haul and clearly an inside job. Thanks to a tipoff a year later, police went armed with a search warrant to the home of a Buffalo Trace employee named Gilbert "Toby" Curtsinger.

Curtsinger had joined Buffalo Trace in 1988 as a warehouseman. During the next twenty or so years, he watched while some of the classier bourbon bottles and barrels he was handling started to fetch

PAPPY VAN WINKLE

Pappy Van Winkle is a highly coveted and collected brand of bourbon whiskey produced by the Old Rip Van Winkle Distillery in Frankfort, Kentucky. The brand is renowned for its exceptionally high quality, limited availability, and cult-like following among whiskey enthusiasts.

The Pappy Van Winkle brand traces its roots back to the late nineteenth century, when Julian "Pappy" Van Winkle Sr. began working in the whiskey industry. He eventually became a prominent figure in the business, establishing the Stitzel-Weller Distillery in Louisville, Kentucky, in the early twentieth century. The distillery produced a range of bourbon brands, including the iconic Old Fitzgerald and W. L. Weller lines, which later served as the foundation for the Pappy Van Winkle brand.

The brand's reputation for excellence grew over the years, bolstered by numerous accolades and awards from whiskey connoisseurs and industry experts. One of the defining characteristics of Pappy Van Winkle whiskey is its extremely limited availability. The aging process for Pappy Van Winkle bourbons typically ranges from ten to twenty-three years, resulting in small batches of whiskey released periodically. As a result, demand for Pappy Van Winkle far exceeds supply, leading to scarcity and high prices in the secondary market.

Pappy Van Winkle has achieved legendary status among whiskey collectors and enthusiasts, with bottles often selling for thousands of dollars on the secondary market. It's one of the most sought-after and elusive spirits in the world. Julian Van Winkle III, the grandson of Pappy Van Winkle Sr., has played a key role in preserving the brand's heritage and maintaining its reputation for excellence. Under his leadership, the Old Rip Van Winkle Distillery continues to produce limited quantities of Pappy Van Winkle bourbon, upholding the brand's tradition of craftsmanship and quality.

astronomical prices. The temptation was too much, and he started stealing bottles to sell and supplement his salary. As he reveals on the Netflix show, he became known as the guy to go to if you want something, and he expanded his business by recruiting members of his softball team, most of whom worked at various Kentucky distilleries. In the end, he had ten other men working with him.

The other guys also devised ways of smuggling whiskeys out undetected. Because there are more than eleven million barrels of bourbon maturing in Kentucky at any one time—or more than two barrels for every person in the state—it's not surprising some could go missing without being noticed for a while.

Wild Turkey was another distillery that lost entire barrels to the gang from Curtsinger's softball team. One of its members was a truck driver at Wild Turkey who simply requisitioned more barrels than he was supposed to, dropping the surplus off at his home before taking the rest to the warehouse. The discrepancies were never noticed. That softball team must have had quite the celebration whenever it won.

The partying stopped when the gang turned on its leader after he was arrested. Curtsinger was the only member sentenced for the crime spree. He was given fifteen years but, as a first-time, nonviolent offender, was paroled after only thirty days under a new Kentucky sentencing alternative called "shock probation." The biggest shock was probably to the guys who had snitched on Curtsinger to the cops. Curtsinger was on parole till 2023 and now works as a house painter. Ironically, he has always denied stealing the bottles of Pappy Van Winkle, which gave the case its name and notoriety, though he admits to other charges of stealing bourbon and handling stolen bourbon.

The total amount stolen by Curtsinger's team will likely never be known, but it must be among the biggest liquor robberies of all time. One of the largest inevitably involves the mob and Chicago. On December 30, 1957, a truck driving from Louisville, the bourbon capital of Kentucky, to Chicago with 875 cases of bourbon on board was hijacked. The cases were divided among various mob-owned bars and restaurants. In today's money, the haul would have been worth more than $550,000. The largest share—four hundred cases—went to the Cafe Continental in Chicago, owned by Gerald Covelli and David Falzone.

Falzone and Covelli had been linked to several crimes, including murder, but this time the police were able to pin the hijacking on them. It's hard to hide four hundred cases of bourbon. However, the jury reached only an 11–1 verdict of guilt, so the duo was acquitted. Later, though, the lone holdout juror who voted for an innocent verdict admitted that he had been paid, and Covelli was later charged with jury tampering.

Covelli was involved in another case of whiskey smuggling in 1962, and this time he turned state's evidence, and three men were sentenced to seven years each for conspiracy. Covelli was in prison himself at the time on charges of car theft. Upon release, he moved to Encino, California. As he left his home there in June 1967, a remote-controlled bomb exploded under his seat and decapitated him.

The Mafia is well-known for disposing of bodies by tying them to lumps of concrete and dropping them into rivers or lakes. A Swiss distillery on the shores of Lake Constance, where the borders of Germany, Austria, and Switzerland meet, attempted to do something similar with gin, with unfortunate results.

The Ginial distillery had been producing its annual Christmas limited-edition TEN Bodensee Gin for three years when something unexpected and nearly unbelievable happened. The process called for the gin to be aged at the freezing cold bottom of the lake for one hundred days, which the distillery claims added a certain something to its aroma and taste. It certainly added something to the cost: the heavy-duty equipment required to lower the gin to the bottom of the lake and to haul it out again one hundred days later isn't cheap. However, when a diver went down to locate the gin and attach the line to haul it back up again, the gin had disappeared.

The spirit was stored in a special steel ball capable of withstanding the pressure at the bottom of the lake, which is 824 feet (251 m) deep at its deepest point, although the gin was sunk only about 1,000 feet (305 m) from the shore, where the depth was around 75 feet (23 m). The container with 230 liters of gin in it weighed 1,764 pounds (800 kg). For security, it was attached to a concrete slab that weighed another 1,102 pounds (500 kg). How can you lose that much gin? The diver made three attempts to find the gin, whose coordinates were of course precisely recorded. The next day, two more divers went down, but to no avail. A commercial diver, Roger Eichenberger, heard about the case and offered to help. He was slightly more successful, as he did at least manage to find the imprints where the container and concrete had been.

The maritime police were called but they admitted to being baffled. They scanned the whole area using sonar and other technology but found nothing. To haul the gin and slab out of the water would have required access to (1) the precise coordinates of the container, (2) an experienced diver to locate it, and, most unlikely of all, (3) a floating crane capable of hauling nearly 3,000 pounds from the lake's bottom. It was a crime that would have been hard to commit surreptitiously, but somehow the thieves got away with it.

The story was embarrassing and costly for Ginial, which planned to produce 395 bottles, each costing 99 Swiss francs (just over $100). Most of the bottles had been sold in advance, and the labels had already been printed. The company reckoned the audacious theft had cost it more than €36,000 ($38,000). That's quite a bill, albeit peanuts when compared to a whiskey robbery that took place in Paris.

The biggest whiskey robbery of all time—that we know about, at least—took place in Paris in 2017, when thieves broke into La Maison du Whiskey on rue d'Anjou in the pricey eighth arrondissement, directly across the street from the British Embassy and only a five-minute walk from the heavily guarded Presidential Palace. The bold and meticulously planned robbery netted the thieves what would be almost a million dollars in today's money (estimated to be €673,000 at the time).

This was another brazen theft in which the thieves broke in through the store's metal shutters and front door at 3:16 a.m. on Monday, November 13. They headed straight to their target and managed to stuff sixty-nine bottles into their bags. One of those bottles, a 1960 Karuizawa from Japan, was worth €195,000 ($290,000) at the time. The distillery that manufactured the whiskey had closed in 2011, and only forty-one bottles were known to exist worldwide. The stolen bottle would be nearly impossible to dispose of legally, since each bottle is

KARUIZAWA DISTILLERY

The Karuizawa Distillery was a Japanese whiskey distillery located in Karuizawa in the Nagano Prefecture of Japan, about one hundred miles (160 km) northwest of Tokyo. It was established in 1955 by the Mercian Corporation, a Japanese drinks company. Karuizawa produced single malt whiskey known for its distinctive character: rich, sherried flavors with hints of smoke and spice.

The distillery ceased production in 2000 and was officially closed in 2011. Despite its closure, Karuizawa whiskeys remain highly sought after by collectors and enthusiasts due to their rarity and exceptional quality. The limited availability of Karuizawa whiskey has led to a significant increase in its value on the secondary market, often commanding high prices at auctions and specialized whiskey retailers.

accompanied by a distinctive netsuke, or gold box, and individually named. It was evidently a theft on behalf of a collector. Despite being caught on security camera in an area surrounded by law enforcement offices, the gang got away with it. The unique name of that 1960 Karuizawa whiskey is "The Squirrel," and the bottle is no doubt now squirreled away in a collector's safe.

One of the most ingenious booze thefts also took place in Paris, and this break-in at a private wine cellar really does sound like a movie script. In the early hours of Tuesday, August 29, 2017, thieves entered the famous Paris catacombs near the Jardin du Luxembourg. The catacombs contain the skulls and skeletal remains of several million people (give or take). Now a tourist attraction, the catacombs are closed at night, but it's known that those of a ghoulish nature can easily find a way in. Secret entrances exist in various places around the city and have been used by people organizing underground parties, raves, and other events.

THE CATACOMBS OF PARIS

The Catacombs of Paris are underground vaults that hold the remains of more than six million people. The catacombs were created in the late eighteenth century to ease the overcrowding of Parisian cemeteries and the unsanitary conditions they posed.

The process of transferring the remains from various cemeteries to the catacombs began in 1786 and continued until 1814. The bones were arranged in a meticulous manner, often creating decorative patterns and displays using the skulls and long bones. It was not only a matter of necessity but also a way to address public health concerns and to create a more orderly and respectful resting place for the deceased.

The Catacombs of Paris extend underground for several miles beneath the city streets and are a popular tourist attraction today, with guided tours for visitors to explore a small portion of the vast network of tunnels and chambers. However, it's worth noting that much of the catacombs are off-limits to the public due to safety concerns and the risk of getting lost in the extensive labyrinthine passages. In all, the underground network of tunnels beneath Paris, of which the catacombs are a part, extends for 180 miles (290 km).

With more than 180 miles (290 km) of underground passageways, it's easy to escape detection or even to get lost. Two teenage boys spent three days wandering the catacombs, also in 2017, desperately attempting to find their way out. They obviously didn't know Paris geography, though the thieves clearly did. One feature of the catacombs is its signs, which indicate the streets directly above. The enterprising thieves made their way to the exact spot where they could drill through the soft limestone of the catacomb wall and into the wine cellar directly behind it. What's perhaps even more remarkable is that they were able to steal and carry away about three hundred bottles of wine. It was no ordinary wine, either, as these were all "grand cru" labels with an estimated value of around €250,000 at the time, or more than $360,000 today. That's more than $1,000 a bottle. No one knows how many thieves there were, since there were no security cameras to record them. We'll just have to wait for the movie.

Another wine heist definitely headed for the silver screen is the ongoing case of a Mexican beauty queen's meticulously planned wine robbery. On October 26, 2021, twenty-eight-year-old Priscila Lara Guevara, a former Miss Earth and Mexican beauty contestant, dined in Cáceres, Spain, with a Romanian Dutch man named Constantín Gabriel Dumitru at the Atrio Restaurant Hotel. At the time, it had two Michelin stars but later was awarded three.

The couple obviously liked the place, as they had dined there several times before. But they weren't there for the food; they were there for the wine list and the wine cellar, one of the best in Spain. On this particular night, they managed to relieve the cellar of forty-five bottles of wine worth an eye-watering $1.6 million. One bottle alone, an 1806 bottle of Château d'Yquem, was valued at €350,000 ($371,000).

So how do you manage to get forty-five bottles of wine out of a cellar without being caught? Well, you start by casing the joint—dining there several times so that you become familiar with the restaurant, its layout, and the staff. This is one way of getting others to lower their guard in your company and to not be suspicious about what you may be up to.

After dining, you take a tour of the wine cellar that is traditionally offered to guests, even if you've done it before. You then return to your hotel room and set in motion a meticulously timed plan. At 2:10 a.m., Guevara phoned the front desk and ordered a salad, asking how long it would take to prepare. The receptionist told her that the kitchen was closed but offered to make Guevara a salad and bring it to the room, which would take about ten minutes.

While the lone night receptionist was away from the front desk, Dumitru went behind the desk and took the electronic key that opened

CHÂTEAU D'YQUEM

The Château d'Yquem is a renowned vineyard located in the Bordeaux wine region of France, specifically in the Sauternes appellation within the Graves region. It's one of the most prestigious producers of sweet wines in the world, particularly famous for its Sauternes wine.

The estate has been producing wine since at least the sixteenth century. In 1593, it was acquired by Jacques de Sauvage, and it has remained in the same family ever since, with occasional changes in ownership due to inheritance. The vineyards are situated on the highest hill in the Sauternes region, overlooking the Garonne River. The unique microclimate, with morning mists and sunny afternoons, creates perfect conditions for the development of *botrytis cinerea*, also known as noble rot, which is essential for producing the concentrated, sweet grapes used in Sauternes wine.

Château d'Yquem produces only one wine, the eponymous Château d'Yquem, which is a blend of predominantly Sémillon grapes with a smaller proportion of sauvignon blanc. The wine is known for its exceptional sweetness, richness, and complexity, with flavors of honey, apricot, peach, and exotic spices. It's often described as one of the greatest sweet wines in the world.

Château d'Yquem is the only Sauternes wine classified as Premier Cru Supérieur in the Bordeaux Wine Official Classification of 1855. This classification ranks Bordeaux wines based on their reputation and quality, and Château d'Yquem holds the highest rank for sweet wines in this classification.

The production of Château d'Yquem is extremely labor intensive and requires meticulous attention to detail. The grapes are harvested by hand in multiple passes through the vineyard, selecting only the *botrytis*-affected grapes at optimal ripeness. This selective harvesting process is what contributes to the wine's exceptional quality and complexity—and price.

Château d'Yquem is typically aged in oak barrels for around three years before being bottled. The wine has excellent aging potential and can continue to develop and improve in the bottle for several decades, even centuries, under proper storage conditions.

the door to the wine cellar. Unfortunately for him, he took the wrong key and had to quickly return it. Guevara had to call down a second time, this time asking the receptionist for a dessert. The receptionist helpfully obliged and went off to find a dessert. This time, Dumitru took the right key and carefully loaded the bottles into three backpacks that he took into the cellar with him. It seems unbelievable that forty-five bottles would fit into even the largest of backpacks, but he did it. We know that because the whole thing was recorded on security cameras, though no one was watching them in the middle of the night.

The pair wrapped the bottles in towels and sheets to protect them and prevent clanking, and at about 6:00 a.m., before the day staff arrived, they checked out and walked off into the dawn. However, the scale of the crime was so huge that it prompted an international manhunt, and the couple was finally arrested in July 2022, when they were recognized as they tried to cross the border from Croatia into Montenegro. They pleaded not guilty, and as of the time of this writing, were awaiting trial, having been refused bail. The stolen bottles have not been recovered.

Almost exactly one year later, in the early hours of Sunday, October 30, 2022, another two-Michelin-star Spanish restaurant was targeted by wine thieves. This time, it was the Coque, one of the most exclusive restaurants in Madrid, with another of the country's finest wine cellars. This time, the gang used the more-familiar technique of gaining access through the building next door.

The thieves first entered the neighboring shop, a pharmacy that had recently closed after the owner's retirement. Once in, they tried drilling a hole in the wall to gain access to the wine cellar, but that failed. They changed tactics, exiting through a pharmacy window into a shared courtyard, smashing one of the restaurant windows, and letting themselves in through the back door. Once inside the cellar, they chose 132 bottles worth in excess of €150,000 ($160,000) from the 25,000 bottles there. The thieves did so without tripping any of the security alarms. Because the restaurant was closed on Sundays and Mondays, the theft wasn't discovered until Tuesday, giving the gang ample time to deal with their haul.

The restaurant owners and the police both believe it was a robbery to order, as the thieves knew exactly what they wanted and took only the rarest wines. One was a demijohn that had been recovered from one of the ships involved in the Battle of Trafalgar in 1805 and would be impossible to sell. Other wines dated back to the 1920s and 1930s and had remained in the restaurant cellar through several generations of the family's owners. Naturally the family was heartbroken.

Not all thefts are perfectly planned and executed, however. At 5:15 a.m. on Tuesday January 5, 2021, thieves broke into the wine cellar of the five-star Domaine de Rymska hotel near Beaune in Burgundy, France. They loaded almost €350,000 ($371,000) of wine into their van, but triggered the fire alarm, which woke the owner, who alerted the police. The van headed south toward Lyon, with the police in hot pursuit. In a scene worthy of the movies, the thieves tried to delay the quickly approaching police by throwing some of the wine bottles at their windshield. None of them hit the target, the van rammed into a toll barrier, and the gang ran off, abandoning their haul. What's remarkable is that only the previous day, the same hotel had been robbed of wine worth €200,000 ($212,000), and the thieves got away. It's never been established if the same gang got greedy and returned the next day for a second round of drinks.

One reason that wine is an attractive target for thieves is because in the past few years it's proved to be a better investment than gold. An organization called Liv-ex, which is like a Dow Jones for the wine trade, tracks the prices of one hundred of the most expensive wines in the world. In 2021, it reported that its index had risen by almost 21 percent, compared to 14.43 percent for the Dow Jones—gold actually fell in value by 4 percent. One wine in particular, a Salon 2002 champagne, almost doubled in price. That's a pretty good return on your money when bank interest rates are low. However, before you start withdrawing your savings to invest in booze, read chapter 7.

It isn't only in renowned wine-making countries like France and Spain that restaurants have to protect their cellars, either, as the staff of the Michelin-starred Formel B in Copenhagen, Denmark, discovered one morning in February 2020. That's when they went to work and discovered a hole in the wall of their wine cellar. It wasn't a big hole, but large enough for a man to climb through and pass bottles to his partner, who packed them. Security footage filmed the heist, which happened between the hours of 4:20 and 5:20 a.m., about two hours after the restaurant had closed. The cellar had a sophisticated security system, though its designers didn't plan for a breach of the shared wall, which was several inches thick. Where there's a wine, there's a way, though.

The hole was from the adjoining building, a wine shop, and the wine shop's stock was ignored in favor of the three-thousand-bottle cellar of Formel B. The target was specifically rare burgundies. Sixty-three bottles were taken, with a market value of 1.5 million Danish kroner ($213,000). It was cruel timing, as only a week earlier the restaurant had been celebrating its prized Michelin star. Apparently its wine list pleased more than the Michelin inspectors. The wines were so rare that when a German wine dealer tried to sell some in Stuttgart a few weeks later, they were recognized and identified as belonging to Formel B. About one-third of the haul was recovered. The wine dealer claimed to have bought them from a familiar supplier— "an unknown person."

A remarkably similar robbery took place in July 2019 at the two-Michelin-star Maison Rostang restaurant in Paris, which boasts a cellar of fifty thousand bottles. Thieves broke in by drilling a hole in the cellar wall, and their main target was also high-end burgundy wines. In particular, they went after the Domaine de la Romanée-Conti vineyard, which comprised half their haul of 150 bottles. As with Formel B, the hole was small—about twenty inches (50 cm) in diameter. Other wines that were stolen included Bordeaux wines from Lafite Rothschild, Latour, and Petrus. The haul was valued at €400,000 ($423,000), though likely much more. As with the infamous 2017 wine robbery, police believe the thieves gained access through the Paris catacombs.

One restaurant owner who had better luck than most is Thomas Keller of the renowned French Laundry in California's Napa Valley. Thieves broke into his cellar on Christmas Day 2014, the day after the restaurant closed for six months for remodeling. The alarm system, for some reason, had been switched off. Thieves hauled away 110 bottles with an estimated value of at least $550,000. Three years later, Keller was able to thank the Napa County sheriff's office, whose dogged pursuit of justice led to the recovery of most of the bottles, which were in a private cellar in North Carolina. When the buyer suspected that the wines were stolen, he contacted his lawyer and refused to make any more installment payments to the seller. Serial numbers on the bottles proved that they were indeed part of the French Laundry robbery, and thanks to wire transfer records, the FBI tracked the thieves down back in California.

THOMAS KELLER AND THE FRENCH LAUNDRY

Thomas Keller was born in 1955, in Oceanside, California. He trained under several renowned chefs, including Roland Henin and Hubert Keller (no relation), and worked in various kitchens across the United States and France before opening his own restaurants.

Keller purchased a historic building—originally a French steam laundry during the twentieth century—in Yountville in 1994. Keller renovated the space and opened the French Laundry in 1994, offering a menu focused on French cuisine with contemporary influences.

The restaurant is known for its innovative and meticulously crafted cuisine, which emphasizes the finest seasonal ingredients and classic French techniques. The menu changes daily and features prix fixe tasting menus, showcasing a series of small, beautifully plated dishes that highlight the flavors of each ingredient.

The French Laundry has received numerous accolades and awards, cementing its reputation as one of the finest restaurants in the world. It has consistently been awarded the highest rating of three Michelin stars since the Michelin Guide launched in California in 2007. Thomas Keller has been recognized multiple times by the James Beard Foundation, including awards for outstanding chef and outstanding restaurant for the French Laundry. It has also been awarded the AAA Five Diamond Award for excellence in dining and service.

In March 2017, Davis Kiryakoz of Modesto was jailed for fifteen months and ordered to pay $585,715 in restitution. In January 2018, his partner-in-crime Alfred Georgis of Mountain View was sentenced to thirty-seven months in prison and also ordered to pay restitution of $585,715. The duo admitted to two other California wine robberies as part of a plea bargain.

Finally, the award for boldest wine thief goes to George Osumi of California, who operated a wine storage business, Legend Cellars. The company stored rare wines in climate-controlled conditions on behalf of private clients, but Osumi started helping himself to some of their bottles. During a four-year period from 2008 to 2012, he stole an estimated $2.7 million in rare wines, mostly from Bordeaux. Osumi was eventually sentenced to six years on several charges, including failing to file a tax return to avoid paying taxes, identity theft, grand theft, perjury, and embezzlement.

To steal the wine, Osumi hired a locksmith to make duplicate keys for the locked cellars, paying him with a bottle of wine, of course. He then pried open the cases of wine, including one that belonged to a friend who had recently died, and replaced the bottles of fine wines worth several thousand dollars each with bottles of the cheap wine nicknamed "Two Buck Chuck" from the Trader Joe's supermarket chain. Some of the stolen wines were worth $3,000 a bottle, so replacing them with wine from Trader Joe's was an impressive return on investment. While it lasted, anyway. But when it comes to criminal activity, none of this comes close to what you read in the next chapter.

· 6 ·

THE WHISKEY RING SCANDAL

Stealing a $50,000 bottle of whiskey or a million dollars' worth of wine is chicken feed compared to the Whiskey Ring scandal of 1871 to 1876. A conspiracy among government agents, politicians, whiskey distillers, and distributors managed to avoid paying what today would be a massive $83 million in liquor taxes. The actual amount at the time was a mere $3 million, and it occurred in and around St. Louis, Missouri. Imagine what a nationwide criminal ring could have achieved. And it's thought that knowledge of the financial shenanigans went all the way to the office of the president, Ulysses S. Grant.

ULYSSES S. GRANT

Ulysses S. Grant was an American military leader and politician who served as the eighteenth president of the United States from 1869 to 1877. He was born on April 27, 1822, in Point Pleasant, Ohio, and attended the United States Military Academy at West Point, where he excelled in horsemanship and graduated in 1843. He served in the Mexican-American War and demonstrated his leadership abilities during the Battle of Monterrey and the Battle of Chapultepec.

In 1848, Grant married Julia Dent, and they had four children together. Julia would become a supportive partner throughout Grant's military and political career. When the Civil War broke out in 1861, Grant returned to military service and quickly rose through the ranks due to his strategic brilliance and tenacity. He gained fame for his victories at the battles of Fort Donelson and Shiloh and for his successful campaign to capture Vicksburg, Mississippi, which gave the Union control of the Mississippi River.

Grant was appointed lieutenant general and given command of all Union armies in 1864 by President Abraham Lincoln. He relentlessly pursued Confederate General Robert E. Lee and ultimately forced his surrender at Appomattox Court House on April 9, 1865, effectively ending the Civil War.

After the war, Grant served as commanding general of the army and oversaw Reconstruction efforts in the South. In 1868, he was elected as the eighteenth president of the United States, running as a Republican. His presidency was marked by efforts to reconcile the nation after the Civil War and to protect the rights of newly freed slaves.

Grant faced numerous challenges during his presidency, including economic downturns, corruption scandals within his administration, and difficulties in Native American relations. Despite these challenges, he remained popular with the public and was reelected to a second term in 1872.

After leaving office in 1877, Grant embarked on a world tour and later became involved in various business ventures, which ultimately led to financial difficulties. He wrote his memoirs, which were published just before his death from throat cancer on July 23, 1885. Grant's memoirs, considered one of the greatest military memoirs ever written, not only secured his family's financial future but also solidified his reputation as a heroic figure in American history.

Grant inadvertently started the criminal ball rolling when he appointed General John McDonald as revenue collector for Missouri district in 1869. McDonald had been born in Rochester, New York, in 1832. Orphaned at the age of nine, he worked odd jobs till he moved to St. Louis when he was fifteen. He was clearly enterprising, eventually founding his own company running a freight steamer on the Missouri River.

When the Civil War started in 1861, McDonald, a strong Unionist, was first appointed a major, and later a brigadier general by Abraham Lincoln. McDonald raised and outfitted the Eighth Regiment, a contribution no doubt noted and appreciated by fellow general Ulysses S. Grant, who at the start of the war had declared that there were only two political parties, patriots and traitors.

Grant clearly saw McDonald as a patriot, although it's a strange kind of patriot who deprives his own government of $3 million in tax revenue at a time when the devastated South was struggling to recover after the war. In 1869, the newly elected President Grant rewarded McDonald with the job of revenue collector for the Missouri district. No doubt at the time, Grant didn't know how loosely McDonald would interpret his job description. Within two years, McDonald's Whiskey Ring opened for business.

In fact, the seeds had been sown during the earlier presidency of Abraham Lincoln. It was then that whiskey distillers across the Midwest began bribing treasury agents to underreport the amount of whiskey being produced and therefore the amount of duty payable to the government. Instead, money was diverted into a slush fund established by the distillers and the agents. Other tricks that were used included labeling some of the whiskey as nontaxable products, like vinegar, labeling it a lower proof than it actually was, which reduced the duty payable, and reusing the revenue stamps, showing that bottles of whiskey were duty-paid when they weren't.

In 1871 the Whiskey Ring, run along similar lines, was established in Missouri with the involvement of McDonald. The revenue collector did indeed collect revenue, but it was for himself rather than the government. This particular crime ring was established by members of the Republican Party, ostensibly to raise funds for the party. In reality, though, the vast majority of the money went into the pockets of ring members. By now other members of the ring included the owners of liquor stores and even internal revenue agents.

The network of people involved went all the way to the White House, as McDonald colluded with Orville Babcock, another former Civil

War general who was employed as President Grant's private secretary. Unsurprisingly for such a large and still-growing operation, the affairs of the Whiskey Ring were becoming more widely known. McDonald wanted the affairs to be kept quiet, and Babcock obliged. Whether the president himself was also involved has never been proven, but it seems unlikely that he could have been unaware of it.

It was Grant, though, who in 1874 appointed the man who would help bring down the Whiskey Ring: Benjamin Bristow. Bristow was a lawyer, a Republican, and a civil rights activist, and Grant's secretary of treasury. He would later become the first US solicitor general.

Bristow had heard the stories about the Whiskey Ring and wanted to send a team of investigators to St. Louis to see what they could find. His proposal, however, was blocked by Grant's private secretary, Babcock. By this time, Grant certainly would have at least heard rumors about the alleged existence of the Whiskey Ring—everyone else in government seemed to know about it.

Bristow was determined to investigate and worked with the US solicitor of the treasury, Bluford Wilson, to find some way of doing so, independently if necessary. They considered moving some of the treasury agents, who were thought to be involved in the ring, to jobs in different cities. Forcing them to move elsewhere in the country could be a first step toward breaking up the ring. This, however, proved to be both impractical and ineffective.

Instead, Bristow and Wilson went underground. With help from the local newspaper, the *St. Louis Democrat*, they recruited an informant and hired treasury agents who were known to be honest and reliable to work alongside him. By April 1875—less than a year since Bristow had been appointed—the team had enough concrete evidence of the ring's existence and activities. Bristow took some of the evidence to Grant, who was unable to act immediately because he had to leave Washington for a while.

During Grant's absence, John McDonald, who by now was in the loftier position of supervisor of internal revenue, heard rumors that Bristow was about to authorize raids on various distilleries and individuals, and approached Bristow to try to get him to call them off.

Instead, Bristow presented him with the evidence, and McDonald had no choice but to admit his involvement.

When Grant returned to Washington, Bristow showed him all the evidence and brought him up to date on everything that had happened. Grant fired the commissioner of internal revenue, J. W. Douglas, on the grounds of criminal negligence. The following month, Bristow carried out his planned raids, and the Whiskey Ring was exposed and finally broken up. In October the trials began in Jefferson City, Missouri, with 238 indictments and 110 convictions, indicating the widespread nature of the ring. Among the guilty were John McDonald, who was fined $5,000 (about $140,000 in today's money) and sentenced to eighteen months in federal prison.

President Grant's private secretary, Orville Babcock, was acquitted after an eighteen-day trial. Grant himself refused to testify and instead sent messages of support for Babcock. The relationship between Grant and Bristow broke down, and Bristow resigned from the cabinet in June 1876. The Whiskey Ring and corruption scandals uncovered in other government departments undoubtedly tainted the last months of Grant's presidency, which came to an end on March 3, 1877. On his last day in office, he gave John McDonald a presidential pardon.

• 7 •

THE HIGH PRICE
OF NONEXISTENT BOOZE

In chapter 5 we saw how expensive some whiskeys are. Even bottles you can buy over the counter can run into the tens of thousands of dollars. They sit there waiting for the guy to walk in with his gold card or maybe for the guy with a trench coat and nerves of steel.

It's mainly whiskey and wine that reach astronomical values and, as always, it's a case of supply and demand. Until we invent time travel, no one can go back and make more of a particular wine vintage or whiskey expression. The supply is limited, unless someone fakes some new old bottles. Which happens, but we get to that in the next chapter. In time, the supply inevitably decreases, through breakage, through consumption, and through theft. Stolen bottles still exist, of course, but they typically leave the supply chain, either by being too hot to sell or by being hidden away in a private collection: most big liquor thefts are done to order.

Over the years, demand for rare bottles has increased. People get richer and want to show off to their friends, or people read about some stellar increases in value and want a bit of the action. And where people want to make money, there are always other people happy to take their money, and not always with honest intent. One such person was Casey Alexander, who took would-be whiskey investors for $13 million, according to estimates by the FBI.

Alexander was clearly a canny scammer. He was British and based in London but targeted elderly people in the United States. This was partly to try to avoid scrutiny by dealing overseas, and partly so he could use his plummy British accent to appear trustworthy. He also invented several companies that sounded respectably British: Windsor Jones, Charles Winn, and Vintage Whiskey Casks.

In all, he managed to deceive 150 people, and probably others who didn't come forward. People are naturally embarrassed by being duped, and some don't even want the police to know how gullible they were. Alexander simply cold-called people, telling them what a good investment whiskey was and persuading them to get in on it if they wanted to double their money inside three years. He even flew to the United States to meet people face to face and reassure them of his legitimacy. He also told them that they would be invited to exclusive whiskey parties in Scotland to further tempt them to invest.

Investors who got suspicious or had second thoughts and asked for their money back were told that the company was being restructured and there would be a small delay. A money-back guarantee only works if the person or company actually intends to give your money back, of course. Alexander's scam started to unravel when an eighty-nine-year-old Ohio man reported to the authorities that he believed he had been scammed out of $300,000.

When police in London started to investigate, they got lucky. Someone working for Alexander who had a previous conviction for securities fraud decided to come clean and spill the beans, hoping to get a lighter sentence for cooperating. Alexander was arrested in June 2022, but the arrest of one man doesn't stop the scams. In 2023 in the United Kingdom alone, would-be investors lost an estimated £3 million ($3.8 million) to fraudsters just like Alexander, openly advertising their investment schemes and then pocketing the cash. In December 2023, Detective Inspector Nichola Meghji, from the fraud operations team at the City of London Police, said:

> As we approach the run-up to Christmas, we would like to remind people of the potential risks associated with investment opportunities, especially around whiskey.
> An investment of a cask of whiskey may seem like a wise choice, and perfect as a Christmas present to some, but we would encourage

everyone to stay vigilant and to not be sucked in—especially if adverts guarantee you will get year-on-year returns.

Certain companies prey on people's lack of knowledge around investment, which is then exploited at a great cost to the consumer.

Or in this type of case, the nonconsumer, because some of the people conned undoubtedly resort to a consoling wee dram afterward. Or perhaps they resolve never to touch the stuff again. The City of London Police offered advice to the public to try to ensure they aren't victimized, which I've expanded on here:

1. Never be rushed into parting with money. Genuine investment companies will never pressure you to act quickly. Most (but not all) fraudsters want you to act quickly so you don't have second thoughts.
2. Seek advice before investing. Talk to family and friends. Someone else might spot something suspicious that you missed. When talking to someone who's trying to get you to invest, tell them you want time to think and see how they react. If they again try to rush you to make a decision, hang up.
3. Try to find out if the company is registered with an official organization. Do not simply accept a statement on a website or a logo on a brochure implying that the company is registered. Do your due diligence and check directly with the organization concerned.
4. If offered the chance to invest in a cask from a specific distillery, check directly with the distillery to establish if the company you are thinking of investing with is an authorized agent of the distillery.
5. Be extra careful if the investment company is located out of your country of residence.
6. If it sounds too good to be true, it probably is.

One major problem is that investing in whiskey is a long-term investment. If investing in a new case of Scottish whiskey, for example, it will be at least three years before the spirit will have matured long enough to be legally sold as whiskey. It's a long time for any return on investment to appear and plenty of time for crooks to disappear. If you're in any doubt, check with the Cask Whisky Association (https:// caskwhiskyassociation.org), an independent body comprised of distillers, bottlers, whiskey experts, and others who specifically combat whiskey investment scams.

These scams have been around for some time, although they have increased in recent years. An early example was the case of Stephen Jupe and the Grandtully Distillery. In the mid-1990s Jupe ran a company called Marshall Wineries, also based in the United Kindom, but he took a different approach than Alexander. Instead of cold-calling people, he got them to call him by taking out advertisements in newspapers and glossy lifestyle magazines beginning in April 1993. He offered casks from the Grandtully Distillery, which he promised would increase in value hugely over the coming years at about 18 percent per annum. He offered to buy the casks back at market value at maturation, or the investors could sell them themselves, bottle them, or allow the casks to continue maturing and increasing in value.

In Jupe's case, he actually did provide investors with casks of whiskey, but they certainly weren't from the Grandtully Distillery, which had closed in 1914. If you think people must be foolish to fall for that, remember that this was in the days before easy searches on Google (founded 1998) or Wikipedia (founded 2001). What investors did receive were casks of bog-standard Speyside whiskey, which were worth one-third of the price Jupe was selling them for. He conned two thousand people out of around £4 million (around £10 million today, or almost $13 million).

It wasn't until 2004, that Jupe was arrested and charged with three counts of fraudulent trading and another charge of using a prohibited company name. That may seem justice was a long time in coming, but the casks had to mature for at least three years, then Jupe's dupes had to try to sell them or contact Marshall Wineries, which was no longer in business. Then the investigations began. After a two-and-a-half-month trial, Jupe was given a five-year sentence. However, the money was never recovered because Marshall Wineries had filed for bankruptcy in 1996 after Jupe had withdrawn large sums of money from the business.

Buying direct from a distillery is usually perfectly safe, but not always, as the case of the Nant Whiskey Group in Tasmania shows. The first thing to mention is that this distillery is still in business but under completely different owners. In 2008, the then-owners did something that is common practice with distilleries. They often offer people the chance to buy casks of their newly made whiskey, which allows the distillery to raise some income while it's waiting for the spirit to mature into whiskey. Some also choose to make vodka or gin, both of which can be made quickly to provide an income stream while waiting for the whiskey.

The Nant offer was a success, and nine hundred people invested money, paying A$25,000 per barrel. Some buyers purchased more than one barrel, and as a result the distillery raised A$20 million. Buyers were told that the distillery would buy the barrels back for A$36,000 when the whiskey had matured in four years, an increase of 44 percent in value. Not too bad an investment—provided everything is aboveboard.

However, what the investors didn't know was that there were some below-board shenanigans going on. It later turned out that seven hundred of the barrels remained empty and never even saw a drop of whiskey. Some barrels were sold more than once, with the first owner's name sanded off the head of the barrel and replaced with the new name. The whiskey in some barrels was inferior in quality and of a lower alcohol percentage of only 45 percent alcohol by volume (ABV). This meant that in the course of four years—once the angels had had their share—natural evaporation would reduce the strength below 40 percent ABV, and the spirit wouldn't legally be whiskey at all. In other cases, the barrels were emptied and the contents bottled and sold, with the owners having not a clue—and not a cent.

It was fraud on an epic scale. In 2015, the distillery's founder, Keith Batt, put the company in his wife's name, which is never a good sign. Later that year, he filed for bankruptcy after losing millions in an unrelated property venture. In 2017, the distillery was bought by a company called Australian Whiskey Holdings (AWH) with the intention

PROVIDING PROOF

The use of the word *proof* in describing the strength of alcohol dates back to the sixteenth century in England. At that time, alcohol content was tested using a method involving gunpowder. The term *proof* originated from the notion that a certain amount of alcohol was needed to "prove" that the spirit contained a high enough concentration to support combustion of gunpowder.

The process involved soaking a pellet of gunpowder in a sample of the alcohol in question. If the mixture could still ignite when exposed to a flame, it was considered to be "proof" of the alcohol's strength. The degree of dilution with water that the alcohol could withstand while still igniting the gunpowder became the measure of its proof.

Over time, this method evolved, and the term *proof* became standardized. In the United States, the proof system is based on a scale on which 100 proof is defined as 50 percent alcohol by volume. In other words, a 100-proof spirit contains 50 percent alcohol, and an 80-proof spirit contains 40 percent alcohol.

Although modern methods of measuring alcohol content are more accurate and rely on specific percentages of alcohol by volume, the term *proof* persists in colloquial use to denote the strength of alcoholic beverages.

of keeping it going, but it was too late for the duped investors. It was AWH that found the seven hundred empty barrels for which investors had handed over A$17,500,000 ($11.5 million, give or take). The case was so complicated, involving several senior Nant employees, law firms, and accountants, that it still hasn't been untangled and no one has yet been charged. With whiskey investing, it's definitely a case of buyer beware.

You'd think that investing money in the drinks giant, Diageo, was a safe bet. After all, this London-based company owns Johnnie Walker, J&B, Guinness, Smirnoff, Baileys, Captain Morgan, Tanqueray, and Gordon's Gin, among others. Diageo distilleries produce 40 percent of all the Scottish whiskeys sold around the world, so surely your money would be safe.

Well, it would be if you invested in the real Diageo. However, in October 2021 a man named Adem Bessim registered a company called Diageo Partners Ltd. with Companies House in London. He used the address of an office he rented purely to receive mail. This later high-lighted weaknesses in the registration procedure at Companies House, where no checks are made, so crooks like Bessim (if indeed that was his real name) can easily create companies that seem reputable.

Bessim first sent out an email that was allegedly from Martin Lewis's Money Saving Expert, Lewis being a prominent British—well, money saving expert. The fake Lewis recommended people invest in Diageo bonds, which guaranteed them 3.5 percent interest. This was a time when regular interest rates in the United Kingdom were less than 1 percent. "Lewis" also said that the bonds "come with Financial Services Compensation Scheme protection." This guarantees an inves-tor's money if a financial institution goes under.

Bessim followed up with an email from his fake Diageo company, linking to a website that he'd had built, describing Diageo Partners as "a prestigious wine and whiskey investment company." The website listed a phone number for investors, although by the time Andrew Penman, a journalist for the British newspaper the *Mirror*, investigated the story in March 2022, the number was out of service. However, Penman found a different phone number embedded in a video on the website (now disabled) that had been linked with other attempts to clone both Wells Fargo and Chase Bank. It looks like Bessim and his partners in crime were revealed before they could do any serious damage. Bessim even left a review on TrustPilot for the company that built his website: "I couldn't be more happier."

It might seem that Bessim did a lot of work for little reward, having invested in registering a company, renting an office, and having a web-site built, but when a scam works, the rewards are certainly worth the risk and the investment of time and money to the scammer. Between 2017 and 2019, two British men made an estimated £76 million ($96 million) from a Ponzi scheme in which they persuaded people to invest in a nonexistent wine. A Ponzi scheme is a scam by which early investors are given an initial return on their investments, which comes not from the alleged investment, but from the money scammed from later investors. The ploy keeps people quiet for a while, convinces them that the investment is genuine, and, if the scammers are lucky, persuades people to part with even more money.

Stephen Burton and James Wellesley operated two companies, Bordeaux Cellars and Bordeaux Cellars London. Through these, they offered people the chance to invest their money in extremely rare wines allegedly held by collectors in their cellars. Their money would enable the collectors to invest in more fine wines at auctions. The borrowers would pay 16 percent in interest, and the lenders would receive 12 percent, paid quarterly. What could possibly go wrong?

What went wrong was that the interest payments ceased in 2019. It wasn't hard to trace the men, since both had been public about their companies, appearing at wine shows to speak about the benefits of investing in wine cellars. Burton was initially arrested in 2019 in a British hotel room, where he was found with two fake passports, some gold bars, expensive watches, and about £1 million ($1.3 million) in cash. He absconded and left the country but was eventually arrested again in 2022 when he tried to enter Morocco using a fake Zimbabwean passport. He was extradited to the United States on December 15, 2023, and was in court the next day, where he pleaded not guilty. The case continues, with James Wellesley arrested in the United Kingdom and awaiting extradition to the United States. If convicted, they face jail sentences of up to twenty years each.

If they do receive their full sentences, the duo might feel resentful, compared to the slap on the wrist John E. Fox received. Fox also ran a wine fraud scheme that brought in $45 million but when convicted received a sentence of six-and-a-half years and was released two years early, in February 2021. He will be on probation for three years. One year was knocked off his sentence for good behavior and the second because nondangerous prisoners were released early due to COVID.

CHARLES PONZI

Charles Ponzi was an infamous Italian-born swindler and con artist who became notorious for perpetrating one of the most famous financial scams in history, now known as the "Ponzi scheme." He was born in 1882, in Lugo, Italy, and emigrated to the United States in 1903, seeking better opportunities. Ponzi tried his hand at various business ventures, including working odd jobs, and even spent time in prison for forgery and smuggling illegal immigrants.

In 1919, Ponzi launched his infamous scheme, promising investors high returns on investments in international postal reply coupons. He claimed to exploit differences in international postage rates to profit from currency arbitrage. Ponzi promised returns of 50 percent in just ninety days or even doubling an investment in ninety days. These extraordinary returns quickly attracted a large number of investors.

Ponzi's scheme initially seemed successful, as early investors were paid off with the money obtained from new investors. This created a facade of legitimacy and attracted even more investors eager to profit from his scheme. However, Ponzi's scheme was unsustainable, because the returns he promised far exceeded any legitimate profits he could generate. Eventually, the scheme collapsed within a year when it became impossible to find enough new investors to pay off the returns promised to earlier investors. Ponzi's operation was exposed, and he was arrested for fraud.

Ponzi was convicted of multiple counts of fraud and sentenced to prison. After serving time in prison, he was deported to Italy. He made several unsuccessful attempts to restart his fraudulent schemes both in the United States and abroad but was ultimately unsuccessful.

According to court documents, he bought "Corvettes, Ferraris, a Maserati, and various Mercedes Benzes." He joined two country clubs and paid for his daughter's college fees. He bought an expensive house in the small and exclusive town of Alamo, where today the average income of residents is $300,000 per year. He also spent almost $1 million on women he met through online dating. He must have kept very detailed records. According to former employees, he also used to park his fast cars in the spaces behind his store that were reserved for disabled drivers.

Fox's scheme centered on a business he founded in 1980, Premier Cru, an upscale wine shop in Berkeley, California. His troubles began in the 1990s, when the store began struggling financially. Of course, by now he knew the wine business inside out. Fox started preselling bottles of wine that hadn't been produced yet. He told his customers (or victims, if you prefer), that a wine bought now for, say, $100 would be worth at least three times that by the time it was produced. They could then choose whether to turn a quick profit, enjoy the wine knowing they bought it cheaply, or stash it away to increase in value. Knowing his business, he chose wines that were well known and desirable but not ultra rare.

When the wines didn't materialize, he would repay the early investors with money he was fleecing from new investors. But as Special Agent Scott Medearis, who investigated the case from the FBI's San Francisco division, said afterward: "Like all Ponzi schemes, though, it was destined to fail, but not before his victims lost pretty much everything."

One customer in Hong Kong lost around $1 million, another lost a chunk of his retirement fund, and one man who had wanted some special wine to serve at his daughter's wedding never saw a single bottle.

During all of this, Fox continued to run his wine shop—and embezzled money from it—but inevitably, as the FBI agent said, it was doomed to fail. Customers didn't receive their wine, because it didn't exist, nor was Fox able to continue returning his investors' money. Complaints accrued, and the FBI got involved. Fox was charged with wire fraud, a common way of charging crooks running this type of scheme. He pleaded guilty on August 11, 2016, and during questioning admitted that between 2010 and 2015 alone he had sold or tried to sell around $20 million of nonexistent wine. During part of his plea deal, Fox agreed to pay back the $45 million he stole from his nine thousand customers. I wonder how he plans to raise the money?

These aren't isolated cases, either. In 2015 another scammer, Spyros Constantinos, was jailed for eight years in London. It's estimated he made £1 million ($1.27 million) from his schemes, half of it from a single investor. It seems you need only to mention the name "Bordeaux" to have people handing over their money to you for wine that doesn't exist. Constantinos's first company, Bordeaux Wine Consultants Ltd., went under, and though not convicted of fraud, he was banned from being a company director for nine years. That didn't stop him from creating new companies and naming himself as a director of them. These included the Premier Bordeaux Wine Company and Classic Bordeaux Wines, the latter based in the Spanish holiday resort of Marbella, notorious as a retirement place for British criminals.

Then in 2016, Jonothan Piper was jailed for five-and-a-half years for wine fraud, also in London. He set up a company, Embassy Wines UK Ltd., which claimed to trade in fine wines. He cold-called his targets and told them he could get top prices for their wine investments. He persuaded his victims to transfer their wines into his company's name, so that he could sell them at a vast profit. He also got them to pay him an amount up-front to cover legal fees, claiming it would be reimbursed. He then sold the wine, pocketed the cash, and the people never saw him again.

Piper's scams lasted for six years, during which time he defrauded people of an estimated £300,000 ($382,000), half of that from a single investor, and he also failed to pay £51,000 ($65,000) in income tax. One elderly woman was persuaded to buy wine from Piper (that he'd scammed from someone else), paying him £33,000 ($42,000). This included £10,000 ($12,700) for a case of Château Haut-Brion 2004 that was being sold elsewhere for £2,400 ($3,000). In a sad commentary on the gullibility of people, Piper targeted many who had been victims of previous scams. He obviously knew that if they had been conned once, they could be conned again. Never be afraid to hang up on a cold caller.

In this chapter, we looked at criminals selling wine that didn't exist or wasn't theirs to sell. In the final chapter, we take a look at some crooks who sold wine that did exist—it just wasn't the wine that they made it out to be.

· 8 ·

IT'S NOT THE REAL THING

When Mount Vesuvius erupted in 79 AD, it buried the prosperous town of Pompeii and its eleven thousand inhabitants. Their bodies decayed, leaving behind shapes in the ash that buried them. We know that some people died in horrible agony because their facial expressions were preserved for posterity. Among the more notorious relics that remained were a kissing couple and a masturbating man. However, we don't really know if that's what they were doing when they died because the bodies would have moved after being buried, due to the intense heat. What we do know for sure, though, is that even way back then, there was a trade in fake wine.

Pompeii, in the Campania region of Italy, was noted in those days for the excellent quality of its wine, which was among the best in Italy and therefore popular throughout the Roman Empire. There was a huge demand for Campanian wine, and archaeologists have discovered that local wine merchants met the demand by buying cheaper wines from other parts of Italy, putting them in local amphorae, and labeling them as Campanian wine.

The Pompeiians probably weren't the first and certainly weren't the last to pass off a cheap imitation as the real deal. Fake wines and whiskeys rank alongside fake Rolex watches and fake Gucci handbags as fertile grounds for crooks. According to the World Health Organization's Global Status Report on Alcohol and Health, as much as 25 percent of booze is not what it purports to be. The European Union (EU) Intellectual Property Office estimates that during any one year, €2.8 billion ($3 billion) in revenue is lost by legitimate makers of beer, wine, and spirits.

THE ERUPTION OF MOUNT VESUVIUS

The eruption of Mount Vesuvius in 79 AD is one of the most infamous volcanic eruptions in history due to its devastating impact on the Roman cities of Pompeii and Herculaneum. The eruption began on the morning of August 24 with a series of small tremors and earthquakes. Residents of the region were likely aware of the volcano's activity, as Vesuvius had shown signs of unrest for some time before the eruption.

The eruption intensified later that day, the volcano spewing a massive column of ash, pumice, and volcanic gases into the atmosphere. The eruption column reached a height of more than twenty miles (32 km). Pyroclastic flows—fast-moving currents of hot gas, ash, and volcanic rock—swept down the slopes of the volcano, engulfing everything in their path. Pompeii and Herculaneum, along with several other nearby settlements, were buried under layers of volcanic debris. Pompeii was buried under about thirteen to twenty feet (4–6 m) of ash and pumice, while Herculaneum was buried under even more debris, including mudflows known as lahars.

The exact death toll from the eruption is uncertain, but it's estimated that thousands of people died in the disaster. Many of the victims were likely suffocated by ash and toxic gases or crushed by collapsing buildings.

Though the eruption caused immense loss of life and widespread devastation, it also led to the remarkable preservation of Pompeii and Herculaneum. The layers of volcanic ash and debris that buried the cities effectively sealed them off from the outside world, preserving buildings, artifacts, and even the remains of some of the victims. The eruption had far-reaching consequences, both in terms of the immediate impact on the affected cities and surroundings and in its long-term significance for our understanding of ancient Roman life and culture. Today, Pompeii and Herculaneum are UNESCO World Heritage Sites and among the most visited archaeological sites in the world.

The crooks don't always get away with it, so let's begin with Operation Swill, for no other reason than it's a great name for a sting operation. The sting started in mid-2012 by officers from the New Jersey Division of Alcoholic Beverage Control (ABC). They suspected that bars and restaurants across New Jersey were serving cut-rate liquor as premium spirits. It's easy enough for an unscrupulous bar owner, after hours, to refill an empty bottle of Grey Goose with cheap bottom-shelf vodka. Place the bottle behind the bar, and how many people are going to know that they're paying premium prices for cheap quality, especially if the vodka's served with a mixer or in a cocktail?

Well, in New Jersey, some folks noticed and reported their suspicions. It seemed to be happening on a widespread scale, from upscale cocktail bars to chain restaurants and dive bars. The investigation took a year, during which time ABC agents attended sixty-three outlets and ordered 150 glasses of neat spirits. They surreptitiously took samples of what they were served. Now, you might be able to fool a drunk knocking back shots of whiskey, but it's harder to fool a lab's chemical analysis.

The ABC then used their new toy, a machine called a True Spirit Authenticator to identify whether a sample is genuine or has been adulterated in some way. For secondary analysis, all samples were then sent to the laboratories of the distillers concerned. Needless to say, they were happy to oblige as both their sales and their reputations were at stake. Of the 150 samples, one in five turned out to be fake.

The next step came in May 2013, when more than one hundred ABC officers raided twenty-nine bars and restaurants across the state and seized more than one thousand liquor samples and inventory records. The officers took away with them all opened bottles of vodka (Finlandia, Smirnoff, Absolut, Grey Goose, and Ketel One), gin (Tanqueray, Bombay Sapphire, and Gordon's), rum (Bacardi Light, Bacardi Dark, and Captain Morgan Spiced), scotch (Johnnie Walker Black and Dewar's), whiskey (Jack Daniel's Black Label, Jim Beam, Knob Creek, and Maker's Mark), and tequila (Jose Cuervo Silver, Jose Cuervo Gold, and Patron Silver).

Among the surprise outlets on the list were a branch of Applebee's and thirteen branches of TGI Fridays. One bar was found to be mixing rubbing alcohol with caramel food coloring and passing it off as scotch. Another outlet, unbelievably, was passing off dirty water as liquor.

Identifying so-called liquor as dirty water shouldn't be beyond anyone with a mouth, but for some deceptions, you need something a little more advanced, like radiocarbon dating. That's what scientists at the Scottish Universities Environmental Research Centre (SUERC) used in 2018 to examine fifty-five bottles of what were supposed to be rare and very expensive Scottish whiskeys. No fewer than twenty-one of them were found to be fake.

The whiskeys were sent to them by Rare Whisky 101 (RW101), a whiskey broker and club. The organization was concerned about the increasing numbers of fake whiskeys being discovered in the whiskey trading market. The fifty-five bottles it sent to SUERC weren't chosen

RADIOCARBON DATING

In simple terms, radiocarbon dating works by measuring the amount of a radioactive form of carbon, called carbon-14, in organic materials. Carbon-14 is formed in the atmosphere when cosmic rays collide with nitrogen atoms, producing carbon-14 atoms. Living organisms, including plants and animals, absorb carbon-14 while they are alive and constantly exchange it with the environment through processes like breathing and eating.

When an organism dies, it stops absorbing carbon-14, and the carbon-14 in its body starts to decay at a predictable rate. By measuring the ratio of carbon-14 to carbon-12 (a stable form of carbon) in a sample, scientists can determine how long it has been since the organism died. This process is called radiocarbon dating.

This method is commonly used to determine the age of organic materials such as wood, charcoal, bones, and shells, and it's an essential tool in archaeology, anthropology, and other fields to date historical artifacts and study the past. And to spot fake alcohol that isn't as old as its label claims.

because of any particular suspicions but were a random cross-section of bottles bought at auctions, from private collections, and from respected retailers. Even whiskey stores can't simply order a bottle of rare whiskey from their usual suppliers; they have to seek it out like anyone else and then hope to turn a profit on it.

By searching for residual concentrations of a radioactive isotope of carbon in the whiskey (carbon-14, more normally used to date archaeological finds or skeletons), SUERC was able to determine the age of the spirit in the bottle. No fewer than ten single malts that were supposed to date from the 1800s were found to be fake, including an Ardbeg 1885. Rare Whisky 101 said that the twenty-one fakes would have been worth £635,000 ($805,000) if genuine, and it estimated that the amount of fake whiskey then circulating in the rare whiskey market was worth around £41 million ($52 million).

Rare Whisky 101 cofounder David Robertson said at the time that every supposedly rare bottle of whiskey "should be assumed to be fake until proven genuine. This problem will only grow as prices for rare bottles continue to increase. The exploding demand for rare whisky is inevitably attracting rogue elements to the sector."

Some rogue elements operated in Spain in one of the biggest whiskey frauds ever uncovered. In December 2020, fourteen people were arrested after joint investigations between the Spanish police and the Spanish Tax Agency. The gang passed off bottles of cheap whiskey as a well-known brand that, for legal reasons, couldn't be named.

The crooks had two bases, one in the town of La Rioja in the province of Jaén, the other in the neighboring province of Ciudad Real in the town of Campo de Criptana, both in southern Spain. The cheap whiskey was made in La Rioja and then was taken to Campo de Criptana for bottling and labeling. When police raided the La Rioja factory, they found 9,550 liters of raw alcohol and 11,200 liters of whiskey ready for bottling. In the other base, they found 36,460 liters of whiskey already bottled, along with an incredible 300,000 empty bottles, 171,200 counterfeit tax stamps, and 27,000 cardboard boxes.

The mastermind was an Asian businessman who imported all the fake items, including copies of the name-brand bottles, from Asia and then sold the fakes to an honest distributor, who unwittingly sold them to bars and restaurants. Police estimated that the fraud would have made close to $1 million for the gang if not intercepted, costing the anonymous brand close to $5 million in lost sales.

It's not only lost revenue and taxes that are a problem; fake alcohol can also be a serious health hazard. The international criminal police organization, Interpol, has reported finding fake alcohol containing products such as antifreeze, nail polish remover, and paint stripper, all of which can cause blindness or death.

The dangers were nowhere more evident than in what became known as the diethylene glycol wine scandal, which took place in

INTERPOL

Interpol, short for the International Criminal Police Organization, is an international organization that facilitates cooperation and collaboration among law enforcement agencies of different countries. It was founded in 1923 and is headquartered in Lyon, France. Interpol assists its member countries in fighting transnational crime, including terrorism, organized crime, human trafficking, drug trafficking, cybercrime, and other crimes that cross national borders.

Interpol operates a global police communications system known as I-24/7, which allows member countries to share information and coordinate efforts in real time. It also provides support through databases containing information on criminals, stolen property, fingerprints, DNA profiles, and other relevant data.

The organization does not have law enforcement powers of its own but acts as a liaison among law enforcement agencies in different countries, facilitating cooperation through communication, training, and operational support. Its mission is to promote global security and public safety by enhancing international police cooperation and coordination.

Austria and Germany in 1985. First you need to know what diethylene glycol (DEG) is, though you can probably guess that it's not a tasty treat. However, it does have a sweet flavor, which is why winemakers were interested in it. But if you drink too much, it will kill you—and too much isn't very much at all. It's one reason you (hopefully) don't drink antifreeze, brake fluid, or ink, or chew glue—DEG is in all of them. It's also been used by mass murderers over the years. Nice stuff!

What it shouldn't be in is food and drink, although some countries, like the United States, do allow it in minute, nontoxic (we hope) quantities as a food additive. DEG has been known to be poisonous since way back in 1930, and in 1937, it was the cause of one of the biggest mass killings in the United States, resulting in the deaths of more than one hundred people. The Massengill Company of Tennessee manufactured an oral antibiotic called Elixir Sulfanilamide. Sulfanilamide itself is a perfectly safe and widely used antibacterial drug. Chemists at Massengill mixed it with raspberry flavoring and dissolved the mixture in DEG. At the time, there was no requirement for safety testing for drugs, so the elixir went straight on the market. The company claimed not to know of the toxic effects of DEG, although papers had been published about it. The company's chief chemist committed suicide while awaiting trial. The following year, the 1938 Federal Food, Drug, and Cosmetic Act was passed, creating much stricter rules about the manufacture and sale of drugs.

Despite this history, in 1982 several Austrian winemakers thought it would be a brilliant idea to add DEG to their wines to make them both sweeter and more full bodied. They all had contracts to sell inexpensive wine of a certain minimum quality to German supermarket chains, but due to the poor harvest in the fall of 1982, the wines were not going to meet that minimum quality level. Rather than lose the contracts, the winemakers "improved" the taste of the wine by adding DEG, which they knew was potentially toxic.

This was bad enough, but some of the tainted wine was sent in bulk for bottling, where it contaminated the German bottling machines. The skullduggery didn't stop, either. Some of the adulterated Austrian wine was blended with German wine, so the poison spread even wider, but, thankfully for German wine drinkers, it was also being diluted.

Although there were no known deaths, DEG, even in small doses, can irreparably damage the brain, the kidneys, and the liver. Once the scandal was eventually discovered in 1985, it ruined the Austrian and German wine market for the next ten years. It wasn't only the drinkers who suffered, but many innocent winemakers lost a lot of money. Many countries slapped an immediate ban on all Austrian wines, and in 1986 exports were down by 90 percent. Some of those involved were sent to prison, others received hefty fines, and one committed suicide before starting his prison sentence. Most of the wine was destroyed, though some was used to make antifreeze.

———•———

We saw in the last chapter how the very name "Bordeaux" appealed to scammers and victims alike. Not surprisingly, as one of the most familiar names in the wine world, it also appeals to crooks who want to pass off inferior wines for superior ones. In the past few years alone there have been at least three high-profile cases of people passing off low-quality wines as top-class bottles of Bordeaux.

In 2015, inspectors from the Institut National de l'Origine et de la Qualité, a regulatory body that's been in existence for more than eighty years, carried out a routine inspection of wines from a company named Sequoia and run by Vincent Lataste in Cadillac, twenty-five miles (40 km) southeast of Bordeaux. The inspectors' suspicions were aroused when they found that the wines, which were being exported to China, had levels of sulfur dioxide that exceeded legal limits. The legal limit is 150 milligrams per liter and these wines contained 150.09 milligrams. It was a tiny amount that easily could have been ignored, but it was enough to uncover a huge scam.

Between 2014 and 2016, further inspections found further frauds. Some wines were found to be blends but were being passed off as from a single vineyard or grape variety. Some wines had the wrong years on the labels, claiming to be from a better year than they actually were. Some were falsely labeled with prestigious names like Graves and Côtes de Bourg. And other wines had simply been watered down. In all, more than ten thousand cases of wine were found to be deceptive in some way. Lataste was handed a prison sentence of six months and fined €30,000 ($32,500).

Wine fraud doesn't normally carry a prison sentence, but this wasn't the first time that Lataste had tangled with the authorities. He had already received a suspended eighteen-month prison sentence in November 2016 for his involvement in another scam. This one took place in 2011 and 2012 (though probably longer) and resulted in the equivalent of more than one million bottles of fake wine being seized and destroyed by the police. The ringleader was François-Marie Marret, who owned twenty châteaus across the Bordeaux region. He used his vineyards to illicitly bottle inferior wine at night, from tankers that arrived at the end of the day to offload their bulk wines. He was given a one-year jail term.

Its desirability isn't the only reason that so many scams are found to involve Bordeaux wines. The Bordeaux wine industry—and the larger French wine industry as a whole—is vigilant about protecting their wines and their reputations, which, in the case of some vineyards, have been built over centuries. So the Bordeaux wine authorities probably uncover a greater proportion of wine frauds than do other less attentive parts of the world.

In a case in 2021, the Bordeaux police exposed a fake Bordeaux wine scheme. In September of that year, while investigating a suspected drug trafficking operation, they also found some fake Bordeaux wine labels. The police's specialist wine fraud unit was alerted. (That the police have a specialist unit devoted to these crimes says something about the scale of frauds involving Bordeaux wines.) The following month, some fake Bordeaux wines were spotted in a shop, and the fraud unit started an investigation that eventually took them eight months and resulted in the arrests of twenty people.

What police uncovered was a scheme in which wines from Spain and other parts of France were brought in bulk to Bordeaux and bottled as midrange wines from the Médoc region, north of Bordeaux. The criminals deliberately did not try to pass cheap wine off as top-shelf wine, instead choosing more moderately priced wine. The head of the gang owned a Bordeaux winery where the wine was bottled, and he was also a wine merchant, which is how he distributed the wine. Police said the scheme involved several hundred thousand bottles.

Yet another Bordeaux scam involved not several hundred thousand bottles but a massive 4.6 million. The scheme began in 2013, and during the next six years, the five people arrested are thought to have made $4 million by buying low-cost Spanish wines and passing them off as various Bordeaux wines. These ranged from cheap table wines to prestigious names like Saint-Emilion and Pomerol.

The scheme began in 2013, which saw a very poor wine harvest in Bordeaux. A cool and damp spring was followed by a hot, dry summer. Hailstorms at harvest time didn't help either. As a result, someone came up with the idea of importing Spanish wines to plug the gap. The wines were imported by one wine merchant, who then sold them to another wine merchant in Bordeaux. With a few strokes of a pen on the paperwork, this merchant changed the nationality of the wines from Spanish to French, and specifically from Bordeaux.

And from Bordeaux to Birmingham—the Birmingham in England, that is, not Alabama—where, in 2021, a store was found with forty-one bottles of fake Yellow Tail wine from Australia. This came to light when a Yellow Tail fan bought six bottles of a favorite wine from the store, only to find that although three of the bottles seemed fine, the other three not only tasted different, but the wines were even of different colors. Enter the police and the Birmingham City Council's Trading Standards team. They very quickly found that it was a nationwide scam, and shoppers and store owners were alerted to the fraud. The wines were confirmed fake by Yellow Tail's owners. It was thought that the wines were made overseas and distributed throughout the United Kingdom by organized crime gangs selling cheap alcohol to unscrupulous shop owners from the back of a van. The store owner lost his license to sell alcohol. One of the attractions of dealing in fake wines and whiskeys is that the punishments don't always fit the scale of the crime.

Wine fraud in Italy didn't begin and end with Pompeii; in 2020, the police in Florence, supported by Europol—the European Union's law enforcement agency—took down an almost identical scam. Thieves were obtaining empty bottles of good quality wine and filling them with the cheaper stuff. They then sold the wines online. Like the wines of Pompeii, these fake wines ended up all over the place, including France, Germany, Spain, and the United States.

EUROPOL

Europol, short for the European Union Agency for Law Enforcement Cooperation, is an agency of the European Union (EU) that serves as the central hub for cooperation among law enforcement agencies across EU member states. Established in 1999 and based in The Hague, in the Netherlands, Europol plays a crucial role in combating serious international crime and terrorism within the EU.

Europol's primary objectives include facilitating the exchange of information and intelligence among EU member states' law enforcement agencies and supporting investigations and operations targeting organized crime, terrorism, cybercrime, drug trafficking, human trafficking, and other forms of transnational crime. Europol operates various databases and analytical tools to support its activities, such as the Europol Information System (EIS) and the Europol Terrorism Situation and Trend Report (TE-SAT).

Two of the gang worked in the food industry, and it was their job to collect the empty bottles from restaurants. Some of the bottles were worth as much as €1,000 ($1,100) if filled with the real thing. Instead, the crooks bought cheap wine online or through companies offering bulk wine at heavily discounted prices and refilled the bottles, reselling them with corks and tops that were as close to the originals as they could find. They then used fake guarantee seals to mask any physical differences.

Their customers were a mix of innocent buyers who thought they were getting a great wine at a good price and those who knew that they were buying fake products, which they intended to sell to someone else at a profit. When they hooked a customer, the thieves followed up by offering even cheaper prices for larger orders.

This is not the only case in which the Italian carabiniere and Europol worked together to bring down wine counterfeiting gangs. In 2017, one operation was uncovered when someone ordered 4,500 wine labels, which aroused the suspicion of the Italian printing company involved. That's the reason most thieves buy their labels and other dodgy items from China, where no questions are asked. The fake labels led the police to find three thousand corks and ten thousand laminate caps for wine bottles. In 2019, the two agencies worked together again, this time finding eleven thousand bottles of allegedly expensive red wine from Florence that turned out to be the Italian equivalent of "Two Buck Chuck."

As a brief diversion and to show what the authorities are up against, the European Anti-Fraud Office (OLAF) once had to deal with a case involving four hundred tons of fake shampoo. Well, it was real shampoo; it just wasn't what the bottle said. The factory in China that made the sham shampoo was raided, but by that time the shampoo was already on freighters on the high seas. OLAF tracked the freighters to make sure none of the fake goods entered the EU.

The freighters stopped at other ports in China and South Korea and then split up, with some going to Mexico and some to Colombia. Authorities in Mexico and Colombia cooperated with OLAF, and the cargoes were confiscated. The value of the shampoo was €5 million ($5.4 million).

Although champagne can come only from the region of Champagne in France, fraudsters in Italy managed to produce fake versions of one of the biggest champagne brands of them all, Moët & Chandon. This happened in late 2015, through one of those accidental discoveries that you often read about in crime novels.

In Padua, about twenty miles (32 km) west of Venice in northern Italy, police financial specialists were investigating financial irregularities at a business that operated a workshop in the city. One of the officers noticed a bottle of Moët & Chandon and picked it up for a closer look. He noticed that the label did not carry the serial number that, by law, every bottle of champagne must have. Further searching of the workshop revealed forty thousand fake labels, a machine to apply the counterfeit Moët & Chandon packaging, and nine thousand bottles of

EUROPEAN ANTI-FRAUD OFFICE

The European Anti-Fraud Office (OLAF) is an independent body of the European Union (EU) responsible for combating fraud, corruption, and other illegal activities that affect the EU's financial interests. OLAF was established in 1999 and operates under the European Commission.

OLAF's primary mandate is to investigate fraud, corruption, and misconduct involving EU funds, including those allocated to EU policies, programs, and projects. This encompasses a wide range of areas, such as agricultural subsidies, structural funds, customs duties, and expenditure related to EU institutions.

OLAF conducts its investigations by gathering evidence, interviewing witnesses, and collaborating with national authorities and other relevant organizations across EU member states. It also coordinates with law enforcement agencies, judicial authorities, and other stakeholders to ensure effective prosecution and recovery of misused funds.

In addition to its investigative role, OLAF also provides support and expertise to EU institutions, member states, and other partners to prevent fraud and improve the protection of EU finances. This includes offering guidance on fraud prevention measures, conducting risk assessments, and promoting good governance practices.

the fake champagne worth around €350,000 ($380,000). Based on the number of fake labels, police estimated that the whole operation could have netted the gang €1.8 million ($2 million). The bottles were filled with cheap Italian prosecco.

Finally, what better way to end than with perhaps the greatest wine fraudster of all time, Rudy Kurniawan, who ignored Bordeaux and focused instead on fake burgundies and eventually got put away for ten years? Among his achievements were offering for sale more bottles of a particular vintage than had been produced, selling bottles of vintages that never existed, and selling magnums of wine dated years before the magnum was invented.

Kurniawan, whose father was Chinese, was born in Indonesia in 1976 as Zhen Wang Huang. Two of his uncles were notorious Indonesian fraudsters, one of them managing to defraud a bank by way of $420 million in loans. Kurniawan changed his name—which derives from the names of two famous Indonesian badminton players—when he immigrated to the United States on a student visa, studying at California State University, Northridge, in Los Angeles in the late 1990s. When his visa expired, he applied for political asylum in the United States in 2001. His application and subsequent appeals were all rejected, and he was subject to a voluntary deportation order in 2003. He ignored this and decided to stay illegally. That's when the fun started.

Around this time, he developed an interest in, first, California wines, especially pinot noir, and then in the wines of Burgundy in France. Later he started buying and selling huge quantities of vintage burgundies, at one time allegedly spending $1 million a month on rare wines. Where the money came from, no one knows, though it's said he was living on handouts from his wealthy family in Indonesia. However, a lot of information about Kurniawan came from Kurniawan himself and thus is questionable. What is known for sure is that this illegal immigrant represented himself as a great expert in and connoisseur of fine and expensive burgundies. He particularly liked Burgundy's most famous estate, Domaine de la Romanée-Conti, gaining him the nickname "Dr. Conti."

Dr. Conti became a familiar face at wine auctions, both buying and selling vast amounts. At one auction in 2006, he sold $24.7 million worth of wine, which was a record for the auction house, Acker, Merrall & Condit, beating the existing record by $10 million. Soon after, things started to go wrong for Dr. Conti, as he grew increasingly greedy or foolish. Now, if a collector sells one bottle of fake wine, it doesn't mean that the seller was the one who faked it. Fake bottles do exist and can be in circulation on the market for some time before someone spots something and cries: "Fake!" But when the same person sells many dubious bottles, people get suspicious.

DOMAINE DE LA ROMANÉE-CONTI

Domaine de la Romanée-Conti (DRC) is one of the most prestigious and revered wine estates in the world, located in the Burgundy region of France. It's often referred to simply as "Romanée-Conti." The domaine is renowned for producing some of the finest and most sought-after wines, particularly pinot noir, in the world.

Here are some key points about Domaine de la Romanée-Conti:

1. History: The history of Domaine de la Romanée-Conti dates back centuries. The estate's vineyards have been cultivated since at least the thirteenth century. However, it was in the eighteenth century that the Prince de Conti divided the vineyard into separate parcels, including the famous Romanée-Conti vineyard, giving rise to its modern name.

2. Vineyards: The domaine owns some of the most coveted vineyard plots in Burgundy, including Romanée-Conti, La Tâche, Richebourg, Romanée-Saint-Vivant, Grands Échezeaux, Échezeaux, and Montrachet. These vineyards are all grand cru, the highest classification in Burgundy.

3. Focus on Pinot Noir and Chardonnay: Although Romanée-Conti is primarily known for its exceptional pinot noir wines, it also produces a small amount of white wine from chardonnay grapes, notably from the Montrachet vineyard.

4. Winemaking Philosophy: The winemaking philosophy at Domaine de la Romanée-Conti emphasizes minimal intervention in the vineyard and cellar. The estate practices organic and biodynamic viticulture, with meticulous attention to detail at every stage of the winemaking process.

5. Limited Production and High Demand: The production of DRC wines is extremely limited due to the small size of the vineyard parcels and the meticulous standards upheld by the estate. As a result, DRC wines are highly sought after by collectors and connoisseurs worldwide, commanding some of the highest prices in the wine market.

6. Iconic Wines: The flagship wine of Domaine de la Romanée-Conti is the Romanée-Conti itself, often regarded as one of the greatest wines in the world. Other wines from the estate, such as La Tâche and Richebourg, also enjoy legendary status among wine enthusiasts.

7. Cultural Impact: Domaine de la Romanée-Conti has had a profound influence on the world of wine, setting standards for quality, terroir expression, and craftsmanship. Its wines are often used as benchmarks for excellence in pinot noir and chardonnay production.

One person who understandably became suspicious was Laurent Ponsot, the head of Burgundy's Domaine Ponsot, founded in 1872. Ponsot noticed that some vintages of his vineyard's wines, which dated years before the wines were first made, were selling at auctions. He began to delve further into where these wines were coming from.

On April 25, 2008, Ponsot attended an auction by Acker, Merrall & Condit that was held in New York. Several of Ponsot's nonexistent wines were listed for sale among the 268 bottles that Dr. Conti was selling. They included Clos St. Denis from various vintages between 1945 and 1971, although the wine wasn't made until 1982. There was also a 1929 Ponsot Clos de la Roche, a wine that wasn't made until 1934. Ponsot believed that most of the ninety-seven bottles of Ponsot wine that Dr. Conti was selling were fake, and he intended to stop the sale.

Around the same time, Bill Koch, the American billionaire businessman and sailor who collected art and fine wines, began spotting an increasing number of fake wines in his own collection. Koch is the kind of man who doesn't buy fine wines purely as investments, as some collectors do. Koch liked to drink them and serve them to guests. Koch hired private detectives and filed a lawsuit against the auction house of Acker, Merrall & Condit, from whom Koch had bought some of Kurniawan's fake wines.

BILL KOCH

Bill Koch is an American billionaire and businessman, known particularly for his involvement in the energy industry, as well as for his passion for sailing and collecting art and wine. He was born in 1940 in Wichita, Kansas, one of four sons of Fred C. Koch, the founder of Koch Industries. This is one of the largest privately held companies in the United States, primarily involved in oil refining, chemicals, and other industries.

Whereas his brothers, Charles and David Koch, gained notoriety for their involvement in Koch Industries and their political activities, Bill Koch pursued his own ventures. He initially worked for Koch Industries but later sued his brothers in a highly publicized legal battle over the ownership of the company, which was eventually settled in 2001 for a reported $1.1 billion.

Bill Koch then focused on building his own empire, primarily in the energy sector. He founded the Oxbow Group, a global energy company involved in the marketing and production of natural resources, including coal, natural gas, petroleum, and related products. Under his leadership, Oxbow grew into a significant player in the energy industry.

Apart from his business interests, Bill Koch is also known for his love of sailing. He financed and captained the winning yacht, *America*³ (America Cubed), in the 1992 America's Cup, bringing the prestigious sailing trophy back to the United States. He has also sponsored numerous sailing events and races.

Koch also has a passion for collecting art and wine. He has amassed an impressive collection of Western art, including works by artists like Frederic Remington and Charles M. Russell, and his wine collection is renowned for its quality and depth—apart from the occasional fake that slips through, of course.

Eventually, authorities realized the large scale of the fraud, and the FBI got involved, raiding Kurniawan's home in Arcadia, California, in March 2012. They found a corking machine, fake labels, stamps, and empty bottles of rare burgundies. Kurniawan clearly enjoyed drinking his expensive purchases but, unlike other collectors, he then refilled and recorked the bottles. He didn't use the cheapest of wines, which would have immediately aroused suspicion, but maybe a $50 wine that he would pass off as a $5,000 wine. The FBI also found detailed tasting notes, including Napa wines that could be mistaken for burgundies, because the swindler took his trade seriously and wanted to ensure that his substitutes matched the flavor profiles of the originals.

No one knows for sure how much money Kurniawan made; estimates of $20 million are probably on the low side. In 2007 alone, he wired $17 million to his brothers in Indonesia and Hong Kong. It's certainly one of the biggest wine frauds ever pulled off and became the first US trial for selling fake wine. The trial lasted nine days in December 2013, and Kurniawan was found guilty. In August 2014 he was sentenced to ten years in federal prison. With time off for good behavior, he was released in November 2020 and deported to Indonesia five months later.

Kurniawan's own wine collection was examined in 2015. The genuine bottles were sold, raising $1.5 million toward victim compensation. His collection of expensive cars, including a Mercedes Benz and a Lamborghini Murciélago with only 938 miles on the odometer, was sold off as well. The FBI raid also found to-do lists of wines that he planned to fake. He clearly took some pride in his work, leaving behind something of a legacy: a film made about his life suggests there may be up to ten thousand of his fake bottles in private collections, still waiting to be discovered. The story continues.

APPENDIX
Legally Binding

As we've seen throughout this book, certain wines and spirits are governed by legal requirements regarding where and how they are made before they can be called, for example, bourbon, tequila, or champagne. It's impossible to give a full list of all legal requirements as they can vary from country to country, but here are some of the more common ones.

BOURBON

To legally produce bourbon in the United States, you must adhere to specific requirements outlined by the US federal government. These requirements are set forth in the Federal Standards of Identity for Distilled Spirits, which are overseen by the Alcohol and Tobacco Tax and Trade Bureau (TTB), a branch of the US Department of the Treasury. For non-bourbon whiskey in the United States, see "Whiskey in the United States," at the end of this appendix.

1. Ingredients: Bourbon must be made from a grain mixture that is at least 51 percent corn. The other grains typically used are rye, barley, and wheat.
2. Mash: The grain mixture (also called the mash bill) must be mashed, fermented, distilled, and aged at not more than 160 proof (80 percent alcohol by volume [ABV]).
3. Distillation: Bourbon must be distilled to no more than 160 proof (80 percent ABV) and entered into the barrel for aging at no more than 125 proof (62.5 percent ABV).

4. Aging: Bourbon must be aged in new charred oak barrels. There is no minimum aging requirement for bourbon, but if it is aged for less than four years, the age statement on the label must reflect the youngest whiskey in the bottle. Also, it must be aged for at least one year if described as Kentucky bourbon.

5. Proofing: Bourbon must be bottled at a minimum of 80 proof (40 percent ABV).

6. Labeling: The label of a bourbon must meet specific requirements set by the TTB. These include stating that it is "bourbon whiskey," the percentage of alcohol by volume, the distiller's name and location, and, if desired, an age statement.

7. Location: Bourbon does not have to be made in Kentucky, but it must be made in the United States.

8. Processes: Bourbon production processes must adhere to federal regulations concerning cleanliness, safety, and environmental standards.

9. No additives: Bourbon cannot contain any additives other than water and caramel coloring for consistency.

10. Registration: Distilleries producing bourbon must register their facilities and their formulas with the TTB and comply with all federal regulations regarding alcohol production and distribution.

CHAMPAGNE

To be legally labeled as champagne, a sparkling wine must adhere to strict regulations established by the European Union and the Comité Champagne, which is the trade association that represents champagne producers. Here are some key requirements:

1. Region: Champagne must be produced in the Champagne region of France. The region is divided into several districts, each with its own specific regulations and characteristics.

2. Grapes: Champagne must be made from specific grape varieties approved by the Comité Champagne. The primary grapes used are chardonnay, pinot noir, and pinot meunier.

3. Production Method: Champagne must undergo the traditional method of secondary fermentation in the bottle, also known as méthode champenoise or méthode traditionnelle. This involves a second fermentation that occurs inside the bottle, which creates the carbonation naturally.

4. Minimum Aging: Champagne must be aged for a minimum period before it can be sold. The aging requirements vary depending on the type of champagne:

   ▪ Nonvintage Champagne: Must be aged for a minimum of fifteen months.
   ▪ Vintage Champagne: Must be aged for a minimum of three years.
   ▪ Prestige Cuvée Champagne: Must be aged for a minimum of three years.

5. Alcohol Content: Champagne must have a minimum alcohol content of 8.5 percent.

6. Labeling: The label on the bottle must adhere to specific regulations, including the use of the term "champagne" only for wines produced in the Champagne region.

7. Appellation d'Origine Contrôlée (AOC): Champagne falls under the AOC system, which regulates and protects the geographical indication of the product. This system ensures that only wines produced in the Champagne region and meeting specific criteria can be labeled as champagne.

COGNAC

The production of cognac, a type of brandy made in the Cognac region of France, is governed by strict legal requirements to ensure its quality, authenticity, and adherence to traditional methods. These requirements are outlined by the Bureau National Interprofessionnel du Cognac (BNIC), the governing body responsible for regulating cognac production.

1. Geographical Indication: Cognac must be produced in the Cognac region of France, which is divided into six specific zones: Grande Champagne, Petite Champagne, Borderies, Fins Bois, Bons Bois, and Bois Ordinaires. The grapes used in cognac production must be grown within these designated zones.

2. Grape Varieties: Cognac must be made from specific grape varieties authorized by the BNIC. The primary grape variety used is Ugni Blanc (also known as Saint-Emilion), which accounts for the majority of cognac production. Other permitted grape varieties include Folle Blanche and Colombard.

3. Harvesting: Grapes used for cognac production must be harvested by hand to ensure the highest quality. The harvest dates are regulated by the BNIC to ensure optimal ripeness and flavor development.

4. Fermentation: After harvesting, the grapes are pressed, and the juice is fermented to produce a low-alcohol wine.

5. Distillation: The wine is then distilled twice in traditional copper pot stills known as Charentais stills. The distillation process must be completed by March 31 of the year following the harvest.

6. Aging: Cognac must be aged in oak barrels for a minimum period specified by law. The minimum aging requirements vary depending on the specific category of cognac:

   ■ VS (Very Special): Aged for a minimum of two years.
   ■ VSOP (Very Superior Old Pale): Aged for a minimum of four years.
   ■ XO (Extra Old): Aged for a minimum of ten years.
   ■ Hors d'Age: Aged for a minimum of six years.

7. Blending: Cognac producers may blend spirits from different barrels and vintages to achieve the desired flavor profile and consistency.

8. Bottling: Cognac must be bottled at a minimum of 40 percent ABV. The bottling process is regulated to ensure hygiene and quality standards are met.

9. Labeling: The label of cognac must include specific information such as the category (VS, VSOP, XO, etc.), the producer's name and address, the region of production, and the Cognac appellation. Additionally, cognac labels may indicate the age of the youngest spirit in the blend.

GIN

The legal definition of gin varies from place to place, and some of the requirements are relevant to all spirits.

Gin in the United Kingdom

1. Licensing: To legally produce gin in the United Kingdom, you must obtain the necessary licenses. This includes a premises license, which allows you to manufacture and store alcohol, and a personal license, which is required for anyone involved in the sale or supply of alcohol.

2. Ingredients: Gin must be made from ethyl alcohol of agricultural origin, commonly known as ethanol or grain spirit. The base spirit used in gin production must have a minimum strength of 96 percent ABV.

3. Botanicals: Gin is flavored with botanicals such as juniper berries, coriander, angelica root, and citrus peel. There are no specific legal requirements for the types or quantities of botanicals used, but they must be natural and not contain any prohibited substances. Traditionally, juniper is the prominent flavor of gin, but this is not a legal requirement.

4. Distillation: Gin is typically produced through distillation. The distillation process must comply with relevant health and safety regulations, including the use of appropriate equipment and procedures.
5. Labeling: Gin bottles must be labeled in accordance with the Food Information Regulations 2014. This includes providing accurate and clear information about the product, such as the name of the gin, the alcohol content, and any allergens present.

Gin in the United States

In the United States, the legal requirements for making gin are regulated by the Alcohol and Tobacco Tax and Trade Bureau (TTB), which is a part of the US Department of the Treasury. Here are some key legal requirements:

1. Licensing: To legally produce gin in the United States, you must obtain the necessary federal and state licenses. This includes a Federal Basic Permit from the TTB and any additional permits or licenses required by your state or local authorities.
2. Base Spirit: Gin must be made from ethyl alcohol, commonly known as ethanol or grain spirit.
3. Botanicals: Gin is flavored with botanicals such as juniper berries, coriander, angelica root, and citrus peel. There are no specific legal requirements for the types or quantities of botanicals used, but they must be natural and not contain any prohibited substances.
4. Distillation: Gin is typically produced through distillation. The distillation process must comply with relevant health and safety regulations, including the use of appropriate equipment and procedures.
5. Labeling: Gin bottles must be labeled in accordance with TTB regulations. This includes providing accurate and clear

information about the product, such as the name of the gin, the alcohol content, and any required warning statements.

PORT

The production of port wine is regulated by specific legal requirements set by the Instituto dos Vinhos do Douro e do Porto (IVDP), the regulatory authority for the Douro Valley and port wine production in Portugal. These regulations ensure that wines labeled as port meet certain standards of quality, origin, and production methods.

1. Geographical Indication: Port wine must be produced in the Douro Valley region of Portugal, specifically within the demarcated Douro DOC (Denominação de Origem Controlada) area.
2. Grape Varieties: Port wine is typically made from a blend of indigenous grape varieties, including Touriga Nacional, Touriga Franca, Tinta Roriz (Tempranillo), Tinto Cão, and others. These grape varieties contribute to the complexity and character of port wine.
3. Production Process

   - Harvesting: Grapes are harvested by hand and transported to the winery in good condition.
   - Crushing and Fermentation: Grapes are crushed to extract the juice, which is then fermented in *lagares* (traditional stone tanks) or stainless steel tanks. Fermentation is halted before completion by the addition of grape spirit (aguardiente) to fortify the wine, preserving the natural sweetness and increasing the alcohol content.
   - Aging: Port wine undergoes aging in oak barrels or stainless steel tanks, depending on the style of port being produced. There are various styles of port, including ruby, tawny, vintage, late bottled vintage (LBV), and colheita, each with specific aging requirements and characteristics.

4. Fortification: Port wine is fortified with grape spirit (aguardiente) during fermentation to stop the process and retain residual sugars, resulting in a sweet and fortified wine with higher alcohol content.

5. Blending: For nonvintage ports, blending of wines from different vintages and vineyards is common to achieve consistency and balance. Vintage ports are made from grapes harvested in a single exceptional vintage year and aged for a shorter period before bottling.

6. Alcohol Content: Port wine typically has an alcohol content ranging from 19 percent to 22 percent by volume, depending on the style and aging process. This is both tradition and a legal requirement.

7. Labeling: Port wine bottles must be labeled according to the regulations set by the IVDP, including information such as the style of port, aging classification, producer name, and the Port Denomination of Origin logo.

RHUM AGRICOLE

Rhum agricole, a style of rum made primarily in the French-speaking Caribbean islands, particularly Martinique and Guadeloupe, is subject to specific legal regulations that govern its production. These regulations ensure the authenticity and quality of rhum agricole.

1. Martinique: Martinique is known for producing high-quality rhum agricole under the Appellation d'Origine Contrôlée (AOC) Martinique label. This designation is regulated by the French government's National Institute of Origin and Quality (INAO). The AOC Martinique Rhum Agricole designation specifies the geographical area, raw materials, production methods, and quality standards for rhum agricole produced on the island.

2. Guadeloupe: Guadeloupe also produces rhum agricole, which is regulated by the French government's INAO.

Although Guadeloupe does not have its own specific AOC for rhum agricole like Martinique, the production methods and quality standards are similar to those in Martinique.

3. French West Indies: Rhum agricole produced in the French West Indies, including Martinique and Guadeloupe, is also regulated by the European Union's Protected Designation of Origin (PDO) and Protected Geographical Indication (PGI) schemes. These regulations further define the geographical origin, raw materials, and production methods for rhum agricole from this region.

4. Other Countries: Although Martinique and Guadeloupe are the primary producers of rhum agricole, other countries and territories in the Caribbean, such as Haiti and Reunion Island (a French overseas department), also produce similar styles of rum. Although they may not have the same specific AOC designation as Martinique, they may have their own regulations or standards governing rhum agricole production.

RUM

The production of rum is governed by different legal regulations in different countries and regions around the world, particularly in places where rum is traditionally produced.

1. Caribbean Countries: Many Caribbean countries have legal regulations governing the production of rum, including:

   ∎ Jamaica: Jamaican rum is regulated by the Jamaican government through the Jamaican Rum GI (Geographical Indication), which defines the production standards and processes.
   ∎ Barbados: Barbadian rum is regulated by the Barbados government through the Barbados Rum GI, which sets the standards and production methods.

- ■ Puerto Rico: Puerto Rican rum is regulated by the Puerto Rico Department of Agriculture, which oversees the production standards and quality control.
- ■ Dominican Republic: Dominican rum is regulated by the Dominican Republic Ministry of Industry and Commerce, which sets the standards and regulations for rum production.

2. Latin American Countries: Several Latin American countries also have legal regulations governing rum production, including:

- ■ Cuba: Cuban rum is regulated by the Cuban government through the Instituto Cubano del Ron (Cuban Institute of Rum), which sets out the standards and regulations for rum production in Cuba.
- ■ Venezuela: Venezuelan rum is regulated by the Venezuelan government through the Ministry of Agriculture and Land, which oversees the production standards and quality control.

3. United States: In the United States, rum production is regulated by the Alcohol and Tobacco Tax and Trade Bureau (TTB), which sets out the standards and regulations for rum production. Although the Caribbean is often associated with rum production, there are also rum distilleries in the United States, particularly in states like Florida and Louisiana.

4. European Union: In the European Union, rum production is regulated by EU regulations that govern the production, labeling, and marketing of spirits, including rum. These regulations ensure that rum produced and sold in EU member states meet specific standards and quality criteria.

RYE WHISKEY IN THE UNITED STATES

Similar to the requirements for bourbon, rye whiskey must contain at least 51 percent rye. Colorings and flavorings are allowed unless it's going to be described as straight rye whiskey. In this case, no colorings or flavorings are permitted, it must be aged for at least two years, and all the whiskey in the bottle must be distilled in the same state (i.e., in Tennessee for Tennessee straight rye whiskey). It doesn't all have to be distilled at the same distillery.

SHERRY

The production of sherry is regulated by specific legal requirements outlined by the Consejo Regulador de las Denominaciones de Origen "Jerez-Xérès-Sherry" y "Manzanilla-Sanlúcar de Barrameda" (the Regulatory Council of the Sherry Denomination of Origin) in Spain. These requirements ensure that wines labeled as sherry meet certain standards of quality, origin, and production methods.

1. Geographical Indication: Sherry must be produced in the specific geographical region known as the Sherry Triangle, which includes the towns of Jerez de la Frontera, Sanlúcar de Barrameda, and El Puerto de Santa María in the Andalusia region of Spain.
2. Grape Varieties: Sherry is primarily made from the Palomino grape variety, though Pedro Ximénez and Moscatel grapes are also used in some styles of sherry.
3. Production Process

   ▨ Harvesting: Grapes must be harvested by hand and transported to the winery in good condition.
   ▨ Fermentation: The grapes are crushed and fermented to produce a base wine, which typically has a low alcohol content.

- ▓ Fortification: After fermentation, the base wine is fortified with grape spirit (usually a high-proof wine distillate) to increase its alcohol content. The fortification process can be adjusted to produce different styles of sherry.
- ▓ Aging: Sherry undergoes a unique aging process known as the solera system, which involves fractional blending of wines from different vintages and aging levels. The aging process takes place in oak barrels called *botas* stored in specific areas of the winery known as "bodegas."

4. Classification: Sherry is classified into several styles based on aging and production methods, including Fino, Manzanilla, Amontillado, Oloroso, Palo Cortado, and Pedro Ximénez.
5. Minimum Aging Requirements: Each style of sherry has specific minimum aging requirements to achieve its characteristic flavor profile. For example, Fino and Manzanilla sherries are aged under a layer of flor yeast for a minimum of two years, whereas Oloroso sherries are aged oxidatively for a minimum of five years.
6. Alcohol Content: Sherry must have an alcohol content of at least 15 percent by volume.
7. Labeling: Sherry bottles must be labeled according to the regulations set by the Regulatory Council, which includes information such as the style of sherry, aging classification, producer name, and the Sherry Denomination of Origin logo.

TEQUILA

To legally produce tequila in Mexico, the process must adhere to strict regulations outlined by the Mexican government, particularly the Consejo Regulador del Tequila (CRT), or the Tequila Regulatory Council. These regulations dictate the production process, ingredients, and geographic region where tequila can be produced.

Here are the key legal requirements for producing tequila:

1. Location: Tequila must be produced in designated regions of Mexico, primarily in the state of Jalisco and limited areas in the states of Guanajuato, Michoacán, Nayarit, and Tamaulipas. The geographical region where tequila can be produced is known as the "Tequila Region."

2. Agave: Tequila must be made from the blue agave plant (*Agave tequilana*), primarily harvested in the Tequila Region. At least 51 percent of the fermentable sugars must come from blue agave. Tequila made entirely from blue agave is known as "100 percent blue agave tequila."

3. Harvesting and Cooking: The hearts of the blue agave plants, known as *piñas*, are harvested and cooked to convert their starches into fermentable sugars. Traditionally, this involves slow roasting the *piñas* in ovens called *hornos* or autoclaves, but this is not a legal requirement.

4. Milling: After cooking, the *piñas* are crushed to extract the sugary juice or aguamiel. This process can be done using a traditional *tahona* (stone wheel) or a mechanical shredder. Again, this is a tradition rather than a legal requirement.

5. Fermentation: The extracted juice is then fermented using natural or cultivated yeast. The fermentation process converts the sugars into alcohol, creating a low-alcohol liquid called "mosto."

6. Distillation: The mosto is then distilled at least twice in pot stills or column stills to produce tequila. The distillation process separates alcohol from water and other compounds, resulting in a higher alcohol content.

7. Aging (for some types): Although some tequilas are bottled immediately after distillation (known as "blanco" or "silver" tequila), others are aged in oak barrels for specific periods. Aging categories include "reposado" (aged for at least two months but less than a year), "añejo" (aged for at least one year but less than three years), and "extra añejo" (aged for at least three years). There is a newer type of tequila called

cristalino, which involves filtering aged tequilas to produce a silver-looking tequila that has the more complex taste of an aged tequila, but this is not yet a legally defined type of tequila.

8. Proofing and Bottling: Tequila is typically bottled at 80 proof (40 percent ABV), though some may be bottled at higher proofs for certain markets or styles.

9. Labeling: The label of tequila must meet specific requirements set by the CRT, including the type of tequila (blanco, reposado, añejo, etc.), the percentage of ABV, the name and location of the producer, and the NOM (Norma Oficial Mexicana) number, which indicates that the tequila meets Mexican government standards.

10. Quality Control: The production process must adhere to strict quality control measures set by the CRT to ensure that tequila meets the standards for its designated category.

VODKA IN THE UNITED STATES

In the United States, producing vodka involves adhering to specific regulations outlined by the Alcohol and Tobacco Tax and Trade Bureau (TTB), a branch of the US Department of the Treasury. Here are the key legal requirements for producing vodka:

1. Ingredients: Vodka can be made from any agricultural product that contains fermentable sugars or starches. Common ingredients include grains like wheat, corn, rye, or barley, as well as potatoes, grapes, or other fruits.

2. Distillation: Vodka must be distilled at or above 190 proof (95 percent ABV) and then diluted with water to achieve the desired alcohol content. It must be distilled to a level of purity where it is "without distinctive character, aroma, taste, or color."

3. Flavorings: Although traditional vodka is flavorless and odorless, flavored vodkas are allowed in the US market.

However, if a vodka is flavored, the label must accurately reflect the flavoring ingredients used.

4. Bottling: The bottling process must comply with federal regulations regarding cleanliness, labeling, and sealing.

5. Labeling: The vodka label must meet specific requirements set by the TTB, including stating that it is "vodka," the percentage of alcohol by volume, the name and location of the producer, and any relevant information about flavorings or additives.

6. Registration: Distilleries producing vodka must register their facilities and their formulas with the TTB and comply with all federal regulations regarding alcohol production and distribution.

WHISKEY IN CANADA

In Canada, the production of whiskey is regulated by various laws and regulations at the federal and provincial levels. The legal requirements for the production of whiskey in Canada may vary slightly among provinces, but there are general standards that apply nationwide.

1. Ingredients: Canadian whiskey must be made from a mash of cereal grains. The most common grains used include corn, rye, barley, and wheat. The regulations allow for the use of other grains or malted barley.

2. Distillation: The wash is distilled in column stills or pot stills to concentrate the alcohol and separate it from the water and other components. Canadian whiskey is typically distilled to a higher proof than Scotch or Irish whiskey.

3. Aging: Canadian whiskey must be aged in wooden barrels for a minimum of three years. The barrels used for aging are often oak barrels, though other types of wood may be used as well. The aging process allows the whiskey to develop its characteristic flavors and aromas.

4. Bottling: Canadian whiskey must be bottled at a minimum of 40 percent ABV.

5. Labeling: Canadian whiskey must be labeled according to strict regulations set by the Canadian Food Inspection Agency (CFIA). The label must include information such as the product's name, age (if stated), alcoholic strength, and the producer's name and address. The label may also include additional information such as the type of grain used, the blend ratio, or any special aging techniques.

WHISKEY IN IRELAND

The production of whiskey in Ireland is regulated by the Irish Whiskey Association and the European Union, particularly through the Irish Whiskey Technical File, which outlines the legal requirements for Irish whiskey production.

1. Ingredients: Irish whiskey must be made from a mash of malted cereals with or without whole grains of other cereals. The cereals used may include barley, wheat, oats, or rye. The mash must be fermented with yeast.

2. Distillation: The wash is distilled in pot stills to concentrate the alcohol and separate it from the water and other components. Irish whiskey must be distilled to an ABV of less than 94.8 percent.

3. Aging: Irish whiskey must be aged in wooden casks for a minimum of three years. The casks used for aging must be oak and have a maximum capacity of 700 liters (185 gallons). The aging process allows the whiskey to develop its characteristic flavors and aromas.

4. Bottling: Irish whiskey must be bottled at a minimum of 40 percent ABV. There are no specific requirements for filtration or dilution, although many Irish whiskeys are chill filtered and may have water added to adjust the final alcohol content.

5. Labeling: Irish whiskey must be labeled according to strict regulations set by the Irish Whiskey Association and the European Union. The label must include information such as the product's name, age (if stated), alcoholic strength, and the producer's name and address. The label may also include additional information such as the type of cask used for aging or the region of production.

6. Geographical Indication: Irish whiskey must be produced on the island of Ireland to be legally called Irish whiskey. The production, aging, and bottling must all take place within the borders of Ireland.

WHISKEY IN SCOTLAND

The production of whiskey in Scotland is governed by strict legal requirements outlined by the Scotch Whisky Regulations of 2009. These regulations establish standards for the production, labeling, and marketing of Scotch whiskey.

1. Ingredients: Scotch whiskey must be made from water, malted barley, and other whole grains. The regulations specify that only whole grains can be used, and no other cereals or fermentable sugars are allowed.

2. Distillation: The wash is distilled in copper pot stills or continuous stills (such as column or Coffey stills) to concentrate the alcohol and separate it from the water and other components. Scotch whiskey must be distilled to an ABV of less than 94.8 percent.

3. Aging: Scotch whiskey must be aged in oak casks in Scotland for a minimum of three years. The casks used for aging must be oak and have a maximum capacity of 700 liters (185 gallons). The aging process allows the whiskey to develop its characteristic flavors and aromas.

4. Bottling: Scotch whiskey must be bottled at a minimum of 40 percent ABV. There are no specific requirements for

filtration or dilution, although many Scotch whiskeys are chill filtered and may have water added to adjust the final alcohol content.

5. Labeling: Scotch whiskey must be labeled according to strict regulations set by the Scotch Whisky Association (SWA) and the Scotch Whisky Regulations. The label must include information such as the product's name, age (if stated), alcoholic strength, and the producer's name and address. The label may also include additional information such as the region of production or the type of cask used for aging.

6. Geographical Indication: Scotch whiskey must be produced in Scotland to be legally called Scotch whiskey. The production, aging, and bottling must all take place within the borders of Scotland.

WHISKEY IN THE UNITED STATES

In the United States, the production of whiskey is regulated by various federal and state laws. Aside from the specific regulations governing bourbon (see above), which has stringent requirements to be labeled as such, there are some general regulations that apply to whiskey production:

1. Alcohol and Tobacco Tax and Trade Bureau (TTB) Regulations: The TTB, which operates under the US Department of the Treasury, regulates the production, labeling, and marketing of distilled spirits, including whiskey. These regulations cover various aspects such as distillation, aging, proof, labeling, and advertising.

2. Alcohol Proof: The TTB regulates the proof (alcohol content) of whiskey. Whiskey must be distilled to no more than 190 proof (95 percent ABV) and must enter the barrel for aging at no more than 125 proof (62.5 percent ABV).

3. Aging Requirements: Although bourbon has specific aging requirements (must be aged in new charred oak barrels),

other types of whiskey are not necessarily bound by such restrictions. This opens it up for woods other than oak to be used.

4. Labeling: The TTB has regulations regarding the labeling of whiskey, including requirements for the type of information that must be included on the label, such as the type of whiskey, alcohol content, origin, and producer information.

5. State Regulations: In addition to federal regulations, whiskey production is also subject to state laws, which can vary widely. States may have their own requirements and regulations governing aspects such as licensing, distribution, and sales.

6. Health and Safety Regulations: Distilleries must comply with various health and safety regulations related to the production and handling of alcoholic beverages, including regulations regarding sanitation, fire safety, and occupational safety.

BIBLIOGRAPHY

Abbott, Karen. *The Ghosts of Eden Park: The Bootleg King, the Women Who Pursued Him, and the Murder That Shocked Jazz-Age America*. Crown Publishing, 2019.

Barbican, James [Eric Sherbrooke Walker]. *The Confessions of a Rum-Runner*. Ives Washburn, 1928.

Batchelor, Bob. *The Bourbon King: The Life and Crimes of George Rebus, Prohibition's Evil Genius*. Diversion Books, 2019.

Blumenthal, Karen. *Bootleg: Murder, Moonshine, and the Lawless Years of Prohibition*. Roaring Brook Press, 2011.

Burns, Robert. "The Deil's Awa wi' the Exciseman." In *Poems, Chiefly in the Scottish Dialect*. Edited by John Wilson. 1786.

Cole, Trevor. *The Whiskey King: The Remarkable Story of Canada's Most Infamous Bootlegger and the Undercover Mountie on His Trail*. Harper Perennial, 2017.

Defoe, Daniel. *Tour through the Whole Island of Great Britain*. 3 vols. 1724–1727.

Dorr, Lisa Lindquist. *A Thousand Thirsty Beaches: Smuggling Alcohol from Cuba to the South during Prohibition*. University of North Carolina Press, 2018.

Gillespie, Malcolm. *The Memorial and Case of Malcolm Gillespie*, 1828.

Guthrie, Thomas. *Autobiography of Thomas Guthrie DD*. James Nisbet & Co., 1874.

Hardy, Thomas. *The Private Papers of Thomas Hardy, 1892–1913*. Macmillan, 1955.

Joyce, Jaime. *Moonshine: A Cultural History of America's Infamous Liquor*. Zenith Press, 2014.

Macdonald, Colin. *Echoes of the Glen*. Moray Press, 1936.

McNeill, F. Marian. *The Scots Kitchen: Its Lore & Recipes*. Blackie & Sons, 1929.

McGirr, Lisa. *The War on Alcohol: Prohibition and the Rise of the American State*. W. W. Norton, 2016.

McHardy, Stuart. *Tales of Whiskey and Smuggling*. House of Lochar, 2002.

Moray, Alastair. *The Diary of a Rum-Runner*. Philip Allan & Co., 1929.

Morewood, Samuel. *An Essay on the Inventions and Customs in the Use of Inebriating Liquors.* 1824.

Okrent, Daniel. *Last Call: The Rise and Fall of Prohibition.* Scribner, 2010.

Platt, Richard. *Smuggling in the British Isles: A History.* Tempus Publishing, 2007.

Rubinstein, Julian. *Ballad of the Whiskey Robber: A True Story of Bank Heists, Ice Hockey, Transylvanian Pelt Smuggling, Moonlighting Detectives, and Broken Hearts.* John Murray, 2004.

Schrad, Mark Lawrence. *Smashing the Liquor Machine: A Global History of Prohibition.* Oxford University Press, 2021.

Shore, Henry N. *Smuggling Days and Smuggling Ways.* Philip Allan and Co., 1892.

Smith, Gavin D. *The Secret Still. Scotland's Clandestine Whisky Makers.* Birlinn Ltd., 2002.

Smith, Graham. *Smuggling in the Bristol Channel 1700–1850.* Countryside Books, 1989.

Stephenson Jr., Frank, and Barbara Nichols Mulder. *North Carolina Moonshine: An Illicit History.* American Palate, 2017.

Thompson, Neal. *Driving with the Devil: Southern Moonshine, Detroit Wheels, and the Birth of NASCAR.* Three River Press, 2006.

Waugh, Mary. *Smuggling in Devon and Cornwall 1700–1850.* Countryside Books, 1991.